DURHAM
MURDER & MAYHEM

DURHAM
MURDER & MAYHEM

RICK JACKSON

THE
History
PRESS

Published by The History Press
Charleston, SC
www.historypress.com

First published 2025

Manufactured in the United States

ISBN 9781467159074

Library of Congress Control Number: 2024949883

There is a time for love and laughter
The days will pass like summer storms
The winter wind will follow after
But there is love and love is warm

There is a time for us to wander
When time is young and so are we
The woods are greener over yonder
The path is new the world is free

There is a time when leaves are fallin'
The woods are gray the paths are old
The snow will come when geese are callin'
You need a fire against the cold

So do your roaming in the springtime
And you'll find your love in the summer sun
The frost will come and bring the harvest
And you can sleep when day is done

—*Rodney Dillard and Mitch Jayne*

This book is dedicated to my brother, William "Bud" Jackson, who has spent a lifetime in service of his community and country. He is the last of his kind who remembers vividly the smokestacks of the cotton mill spilling white smoke skyward and the smell of Bright leaf tobacco filling the air around the red brick buildings downtown. He is, to his core, "Old Durham" and my hero.

CONTENTS

CONTENTS

INTRODUCTION

Durham was not a city until 1869, and even then it was located in Orange County. Durham County didn't exist until another twelve years later, in 1881. The area had been settled since the 1750s due to the fertile lowlands around the Eno, Flat and Little Rivers. Lying between Hillsborough, Chapel Hill and Raleigh, the wagon trails eventually turned into railroad lines. This region immediately gained a reputation as a tough area. Professor John Spencer Bassett would later say of Pin Hook, as he compiled the city's history, "The shiftless of society, usually addicted to vices of one sort or another, tended to congregate there, attracting others of their kind. A rough and brawling place with grog shops, and brothels, it offered wagoners a campground and a well along with its other attractions." Land was bought from Bennett Durham to build a rail station in an area that would become known as Pin Hook in today's West Durham.

The boom did not come to Durham until after the Civil War, when Confederate General Joseph Johnston surrendered the remaining Confederate forces to General Sherman at the Bennett Farm. The war was over, but the veterans went home with many of the habits they had formed while in the service. Bright leaf tobacco became a hot commodity across the country and the world. The Duke family capitalized on this and soon found themselves among the wealthiest families in the country. They founded Trinity College, later Duke University, and Watts Hospital.

After the war, the African American community also found opportunities in Durham that other places denied. The National Religious Training

Durham, the Bull City, has a duel reputation as a city of growth and innovation, as well as a city that struggles with crime. *Author's collection.*

School at Chautauqua was founded and would go on to become North Carolina Central University. Lincoln Hospital was established, and so was North Carolina Mutual Life, which for much of the twentieth century was the largest Black-owned institution in the world. Durham became known as the "Black Wall Street," a name shared with Tulsa, Oklahoma. Unlike Tulsa, which suffered a brutal race riot and massacre, Durham was able to continue to thrive and expand the African American community into the present day.

Though originally a blue-collar city, Durham has shifted in the last few decades after the tobacco industry fell and textiles mills moved south. Durham is now a haven for tech and medical jobs and is known as the "City of Medicine." People come from around the world to receive care in the many hospitals and to share research. The Durham Bulls, the minor-league baseball team made famous by the movie *Bull Durham*, has given the city another nickname, the "Bull City." So many great attributes draw many from around the country to live in Durham, but the Bull City has still not totally shed the reputation it received from back in the Pin Hook days. Crime is still a real problem that festers under the surface of the city every day. Local news channels vacillate between stories of sports accolades, business growth and medical innovation on the one hand and murder, robbery and rape on the other.

Several famous cases have made their way to the national news. The murder of author Michael Peterson's wife has been chronicled in books, documentaries and in a television miniseries. The nation watched the accusations of the Duke lacrosse team come unraveled, causing the lead prosecutor and district attorney to resign, be disbarred and serve time in prison for ethics violations. There were many more instances of murder and mayhem in the City of Medicine. From the time the first settlement formed in the low grounds along the rivers to today, crime has been a staple part of the very fibers of Durham.

SERGEANT GILL CATES

Felix Conklin's wife had had enough. Enough of the beatings and the cursings. Enough of not having enough money to feed her three kids. Enough of their sorry father bringing shame to their family around town. Her husband had been on a weeklong bender when she finally decided enough was enough in May 1913. She took her kids and a few belongings down Chatham Street to a friendly neighbor's home, where she was allowed to board a room. The Smiths were good people and had seen firsthand the way Felix Conklin treated his family, and it was more than enough for them to offer help.

Felix was known around Durham as a drunk and had become a frequent guest in the jailhouse, mostly due to the brutal beatings that he would lay on his wife and kids. He worked odd jobs around town in markets and livery stables. But he could not hold a job for long before not showing up for extended stretches or, worse, showing up drunk and belligerent.

It was the night of May 28 when he finally sobered up enough to realize that they were gone. He thought he knew where they would be, so he grabbed his .44-caliber pistol and shoved it in his pocket, covering it up with his jacket, and then headed toward the Smiths' house. He staggered onto the porch and began to beat on the door. Mr. Smith was not home, and Mrs. Smith eased her way to the door.

She could see the fear on the face of Mrs. Conklin as she stood in front of her children, but she tried to reassure them that everything was going to be okay with a wave of the hand. Mrs. Smith was sure that Felix would not

Above: Durham Police Sergeant Gil Cates (*center back row*) became the first officer killed in the line of duty in Durham. *Durham Newspapers.*

Left: Officer Gill Cates worked out of Durham's first courthouse. *Durham County Library, North Carolina Collection.*

be so foolish as to try to force himself into her home to get at his wife and kids. She opened the door and came face to face with him on her porch. In an instant, as he looked past her and saw his wife, he produced his pistol and fired it over her shoulder. Mrs. Smith, startled by the loud bang of the revolver by her ear, slammed the door shut in his face, and they all took cover on the floor of her house. Mrs. Conklin cried out in pain, and Mrs. Smith could see that there was a large hole in her leg that was gushing blood and creating a pool on the floor. The children screamed and cried as more shots rang out and hit the door and the front of the house.

Mrs. Smith crawled over to Mrs. Conklin and began to wrap her wound in a towel. Finally, the shooting stopped, and silence broke over the house. They waited breathlessly for several minutes before daring to even speak. The women decided to wait until they knew he was gone and send one of the kids to a neighbor's house, where they could use a phone to call for help. About a half hour later, they sent one of the older girls, who ran the one thousand yards to the neighbor's house in record time.

When the call for help came into the police station, Sergeant Gill Cates was on his way out the door to make an arrest on the other side of town with

Sergeant Cates was ambushed by a very intoxicated Felix Conklin in 1913. *From the Durham Recorder.*

another officer. It would have to wait, though, and they headed out toward Chatham Street to find Felix. On the way out, they ran into Sheriff's Deputy Lonnie Morgan, who was told to go along with them and help make the arrest by Sheriff Harward.

When they got to the Smith house, Mrs. Conklin was already at the hospital getting treatment. They talked to the very shaken Mrs. Smith, and there was no doubt who they were after then. They searched the area around the house, but he was long gone so they headed toward the Conklin residence.

As they approached the house, they saw a man sitting on the front porch with a blanket over his lap. Although Felix Conklin was a known problem in town, none of the three law enforcement officers there knew him by sight. Cates took the lead as they walked toward the house.

"Who lives here?" he asked.

"I live here," Conklin replied through a scowl.

"Does C.F. Conklin live here?" Cates asked as he reached the steps.

"I am C.F. Conklin," he replied.

Cates was reaching out to take his shoulder when, suddenly, Conklin slipped his hand under the blanket on his lap, pulled out his pistol and shot Cates point-blank in the chest. Cates staggered back down the steps and fell under a tree. As he fell, he yelled out, "Don't let him get away, he has killed me!"

Deputy Morgan pulled his own revolver from his coat pocket and fired five shots at Conklin, hitting him three times in the chest, killing him. Morgan ran up on the porch and kicked the gun away from the slumping body of Conklin and turned to help Cates. As he and the other officer dragged Cates toward the road, the sheriff pulled up in a buggy. Luckily, he had come after them to assist with the arrest himself. Now he was acting as an ambulance to get Cates to the hospital as fast as possible.

It was no use though. Cates had been shot through the right lung. The bullet had created such a large hole that the doctors could not save his life. He died within a half hour after arriving at the hospital. He left behind a young, grieving widow but no children. All of his fellow officers mourned along with her and said that he had been a great police officer. Inscribed on his headstone were these words:

Loyal to His Friends
Lenient to His Enemies
And Faithful to His Duties

THE EXECUTION OF WILLIE BELL

On the night of March 8, 1915, merchant B.N. Mann walked out of his store on Fayetteville Street, wishing his clerk a good night, and headed down the street toward his home. He was next seen by a pedestrian lying in a pool of blood on the corner of Dillard and Peabody Streets. He was carried to the hospital and died less than two hours later. Police descended on the scene to try to find any clues to who could have committed the crime and found a broken pool cue. Later, another officer found the other piece to the broken cue behind a billboard across from the Thomas-Howard Grocery Store on Peabody Street. They could find no one who had witnessed the crime and had few leads.

A few days later, two police officers arrested Willie Bell for vagrancy and then released him a few days later. He was a twenty-year-old man who had come to Durham as a child and had more than one run-in with the Durham police and Sheriff's Department in the past few years. He was initially not thought to be a suspect in the death of Mr. Mann, but the police had been working their sources in the community. A picture began to emerge that led them to re-arrest Willie Bell and charge him with murder.

Bell initially claimed his innocence and pleaded not guilty to all chargers, but soon he changed his tune hoping to get a lighter sentence. He confessed to the sheriff and a jailer and then repeated his confession to a writer with the *Durham Herald* newspaper. What he confessed confirmed what evidence the police had gathered and filled in some of the holes in the information they had.

According to Bell, on the night of March 8, he left his house around 7:00 p.m. and went to Burnett's Pool Hall, where he played pool for a while and then left to head back home. Carrying his own pool cue, he saw a man standing on the corner of Dillard and Peabody. He crept up behind the man and struck him once on the head. The man fell, and Willie Bell rifled through his pockets, taking fifteen dollars and then running off.

Bell saw that the blow had broken his cue, so he tossed the piece he still had behind the billboard and continued toward home. As he went along, he began to fear getting caught. He tossed the pocketbook that he had taken from Mr. Mann under a house on McMannen Street and headed back toward the pool hall, where he told Burnett's employee George Norwood what he had done and gave him fifty cents for another pool cue to replace the one he had used to kill Mr. Mann. Bell made Norwood swear that he would not tell anyone what he had told him.

Bell left the pool hall and found a friend of his, Eddie Bumpass. Bell gave him money and asked him to hold it for him. Bell didn't tell Bumpass where he had gotten the money, but Bumpass would later testify that Bell indicated with a wink and a nod that the money was stolen.

In the time between when the murder occurred and when Bell was arrested for the crime, he swore that he had not told a soul but Norwood, yet people all around the area testified that Bell told several people and talked openly about it. He was spending money up and down Mangum Street, which was not typical and was noticed by the people who knew him.

Bell's hope for mercy in confessing was soon shattered, as he was sentenced to death, to take place on July 8, 1915. Just a short four months after the murder of Mr. Mann, Willie Bell was strapped into the state's electric chair. Reverend James Satterwhite read quietly from the Bible as they strapped Bell's hands and feet into the chair.

"What was that last verse you read?" Bell asked, suddenly breaking his silence.

"Lord Jesus, have mercy upon me," the reverend said.

"Yes, that's right. I don't want to forget it. Lord Jesus, have mercy upon me."

The men went back to their work and finished strapping him into the chair. They left the room, and at 10:30 a.m., a bolt of electricity was sent through his body. One jolt was enough, and before five minutes had passed, Willie Bell was dead.

The night before his execution, he asked if he could be taken around the cell block to speak to the other inmates and tell them to repent of their sins. He had requested to see his brother, Walter Bell, before he died, which was granted. As they led him from his cell to the execution chamber, the inmates sang "Jesus Paid It All." In his last moments, Willie Bell had wanted to save as many as he could from the fate that awaited him. His last request was for Reverend R. Spiller of Mount Vernon Church in Durham to give a sermon in the courthouse square. Spiller made the request to the city, and it was approved. When Spiller spoke that Sunday, he delivered the message that Bell had requested. To a large crowd of men and women, Black and white, the good reverend preached a sermon about turning away from drugs, whiskey and crime—don't let these things entrap you as they had Willie Bell. Hopefully, someone in the crowd got the message that day and a life was saved.

THE AMBUSH OF ROBERT JONES

Robert Jones walked swiftly along the old southern road toward home on a cold February night in 1918. Work was hard in the city, and it was not easy to find good-paying work at that. But he worked from dawn to dusk at any job he could get around the Bull City in an effort to bring home enough to satisfy his wife, Geneva. He was right on time as he neared the East Station. He expected to see people waiting around the station, but it looked empty. Since the United States had entered the Great War in Europe, Durham had been a busy place, but the cold wind cut through the darkness that night and made him feel alone. As he reached the coal chute by the station, he passed by a hidden figure who stepped out of the shadows as he passed. The figure raised a broomstick and struck Robert across the back of the head.

Robert, stunned, spun around and faced his attacker. He could see no features, just a dark figure. Jones saw the figure raise the stick again over his head, but he was too dazed to protect himself as the figure brought the stick down again on his head. Robert Jones stumbled back and finally toppled over, his eyes glazed over, staring up at the black sky. The breath of the attacker formed in front of him like a bull as he looked down at his victim. The vapor of breath coming from Robert Jones grew weaker and weaker as life drained away from him. A moment later, his slayer crept back into the shadows and began to run into the night, heading out of town.

It didn't take the police long to find their man. Geneva Jones was known to be in a long-term intimate relationship with a man named Lonnie Council.

It seemed everyone knew. Probably even Robert knew, but day after day, he went off to work to try to please Geneva. Lonnie was found at a wood cutting camp six miles outside Durham, where he confessed to the crime immediately. Justice, usually brutally swift in this era, was delayed by his confession. He told the sheriff that he had attacked Robert Jones, but had done so at the direction of Robert's wife, Geneva. Council told them that they had been involved for two years and the previous week had seen each other at Geneva's sister's funeral. Geneva had pulled him aside, away from prying eyes and ears, and told him that now was the time to get Robert out of the way for good so that they could be together.

She was a woman with a dynamic personality, and Lonnie was utterly under her control, he told the deputies who arrested him. She had explained to Lonnie the route that Robert took home every night and told him where he could hide to not be seen by Robert as he passed, nor seen by any witnesses. Lonnie told them that she had told him what weapon to use and how to wait for him to pass before he struck him from behind. As they took Lonnie into custody, they decided that his accusation was convincing enough to take her into custody for being an accessory before the fact. They talked to the men in the camp, and no one had seen him the day before between 4:30 p.m. and around 9:00 p.m. Upon further investigation, they discovered that Geneva Jones had recently taken out a $200 life insurance policy on Robert. When Geneva was taken into custody, she denied everything. She denied the affair and denied planning the murder with or for Lonnie Council.

They jailed them both—Lonnie waiting for his death and Geneva waiting for her trial. Lonnie Council's execution was postponed so that he could testify against Geneva, which he did. At the conclusion of the trial, the attorney who represented Geneva argued that the testimony of Lonnie should be struck from the record because he was "officially dead" since he had passed the date of his execution. The court ruled that an "official death" did not trump presence in the flesh, and the motion was denied. The Hail Mary pass failed to win the game for the defense, and she was sentenced to life in prison. The sentence was commuted to ten years in prison by Governor Bickett. It was reflection of the attitude of the time of giving more grace when it came to the punishment of women in cases like this and also due to the fact that even if the crime had been committed at her behest, it was Lonnie Council who had swung the fatal blows.

On June 7, 1918, Lonnie Council was led into the cold, octagon-shaped room of the state prison where sat the electric chair. Asked if he would like to make a statement before his death, he just shook his head. Eyes and head down, he was led to the chair and strapped in. As the men worked around him preparing his execution, he sat quietly and waited for his fate. Moments later, the switch was engaged, and Lonnie Council was gone. Some would say that he was led astray by an evil woman, but others would say that he paid for the crime that he chose to commit. In the end, it did not matter. He paid the price for what he did, and the question of blame was left to his maker.

THE STRANGE CASE OF ROBERT WILES

Robert "Bob" Wiles stood outside of a rooming house on Chapel Hill Street on August 8, 1925. He vacillated between being in a daze and feeling like he was going to jump out of his skin. It seemed like a hive of bees were in his belly as he waited on the street in an alcove partially hidden from view. People passed by mostly without even noticing him, but it was not the hot Carolina sun he was hiding from. He needed to be unseen to do what he had come for. Soon, he saw her. A car pulled up in front of the rooming house, and a woman and man stepped out. The bees in his stomach seemed to come together into a weight that dropped to the bottom of his stomach. He felt his heart breaking in his chest. To know and to see are very different things. He knew that his wife, Drom, had left him and ran off with Ralph Gordon, but there they were. He thought of his two daughters at home with his mother, where she had left them when she ran off. He put his hands in his jacket pocket and followed behind them.

They climbed the stairs in front of him and reached the door as he came up behind them. As Ralph Gordon turned to close the door, he was surprised by a foot wedged in between the door and the frame. Suddenly, the door flung open, and Ralph stepped back. Bob appeared with a pistol in hand.

"Now, what is this?" he shouted.

Ralph reached into his pocket, and Bob began to fire into him. Ralph reached behind him and grabbed Drom to steady himself as he fell but instead pulled her in front of him as the shots rang out. Bob's rage halted as he saw her wince in pain from a shot. He threw the pistol on the bed and grabbed her. He carried her down the stairs yelling for help, and she was taken to Watts Hospital, where she soon died. Before she had passed, Bob Wiles was already taking up residency at the Durham County Jail, charged with the murder of Ralph Gordon. As soon as his wife passed, he was also charged with her death. Over the next two months, while he waited for trial, the newspapers carried the story of the crime, and the people of Durham became enamored of the case. It was sensational. It was a story of a love triangle and a wronged husband left with two little girls to raise while his wife left them all for her lover. Most people felt that the "unwritten law" applied ("an outraged husband, father, or brother could justifiably kill the alleged libertine who had been sexually intimate with the defendant's wife, daughter, or sister").

Bob Wiles came to Durham in 1925 to search for his wayward wife and her lover. *From the* Columbia Record.

Wiles was to be tried separately for the murders since he had planned to kill Gordon, but it was believed that he killed his wife in error as a crime of passion. When it came time for the trial, the men of the jury heard the case, and little was disputed. The Honorable Judge Grady presided and made a point to tell the jury as they went into chambers that in North Carolina, there was no such thing as the "unwritten law" and that they should judge the case on the letter of the law as it is written.

The jury took an initial vote, which was eleven to one, not guilty. The holdout stuck to his opinion and belief that the judge was right. There should be no unwritten law, and they needed to proceed with the law on the books. They deliberated late into the night, and the lone dissenting juror asked if he could sleep on it. He slept little that night, and early in the morning, he let the jury foreman know that he had made his decision. The foreman would find out later that morning whether he would either vote not guilty or if the jury would be hung.

At seven o'clock in the morning, the red-eyed jury shuffled into the jury box as the judge and people in the courtroom looked on. The accused Robert Wiles, with his father and his lawyer by his side, stood waiting for the verdict. Waiting as well was Paul Gordon, the son of the slain man.

Judge Grady cleared his throat, "Gentlemen, are you agreed upon a verdict?"

"We are, sir," answered the jury foreman.

"How say you in the case of Robert H. Wiles? Is he guilty or not guilty?"

"Not guilty," came the reply from the weary foreman. A low murmur filled the courtroom as the judge continued.

"Not guilty, so say you all?" The men of the jury nodded in unison as the foreman answered in the affirmative.

Robert Wiles leaped to his feet upon the final affirmation of the jury. He walked toward the jury box and began to shake the hand of each man who had voted for his freedom. "Gentleman of the jury, I want to thank you, everyone. God bless you all." When he had finished, he walked to the judge and shook his hand also, thanking him for presiding over a fair and impartial trial. He then embraced his father and shook the hand of his lawyer. Less than ten feet away sat Paul Gordon, stoically watching the scene. Newly minted as a U.S. marine, he sat in his dress uniform, standing out among the crowd. He clearly loved his father, and no matter the circumstance of the killing, he wanted to see some form of justice applied to Wiles.

Robert Wiles had won his fight for the murder of Ralph Gordon, but he was still under indictment for the murder of his wife. Judge Henry Grady brought the court back in order and reminded Wiles of this fact. He would be allowed to return to Columbia, but he had to return to stand trial for her death. Robert Wiles's mood changed, and he stood listening to the judge. When asked if he wanted to make a statement, he spoke clearly for everyone to hear:

> *The one thing I regret was killing my wife. I had no intention of harming her. Gordon swung her into the path of my bullets before I could stop firing. When I saw she was hit, I threw the gun upon the bed and grabbed her up. But, it was too late then, and for the children's sake, I am sorry....However, they will be with my mother, where they are now. I will do my best to bring them up right. I am going back now to work for them and to show, by my life, that the people of North Carolina were right when they turned me loose. I believe, even now, that my two little girls are better off safe in Columbia, under proper care, than they would have been even with their mother, if another man was there too.*

When he left the courtroom, Wiles went straight to the newspaper and made a comment thanking the people of Durham and North Carolina for their support during his time in jail. During his ten weeks in the Durham County Jail, he had become a sort of cultural hero to many. He had been lush with chewing tobacco and food from citizens who made daily deliveries for him. He left for Columbia immediately after, back to his little girls. Wiles soon found out that shortly after the trial, superior judges in North Carolina had been convened to discuss the charges of the murder of his wife. They decided to proceed "nol-pros," meaning they were unwilling to prosecute, and the charges for her murder were dropped. Wiles breathed a sigh of relief and set out to live a new life.

Unfortunately for Wiles and for many others, a dark cloud formed over him and seemed to follow him until the end. Just a few months after the ruling, Bob Wiles's brother, who was also an auto mechanic and a fairly well-known racecar driver in South Carolina, was killed in a crash at a Labor Day race event. Bob married the young Callie Frick and tried to get back to a normal life. He found himself unable to find or keep employment, although he was known as someone who was a talented mechanic and a pleasant man to be around. He could just never make it work.

By Christmas 1934, he found himself unemployed with a three-year-old, Robert Jr., and his wife had informed him that she was going to have another baby soon. His two daughters were grown by then, but at forty-nine years old and unemployed, he felt an immense pressure. He developed a plan to kidnap the son of a local grocery magnate, H.H. Harris, and ask for a reward of $10,000. He decided later that he could not possibly ask for that much. Wiles knew from his own misery that things could be bad financially for Mr. Harris, and he would not be able to pay that much. He decided to ask for only $1,000, and two days before Christmas, he put his plan into effect.

Wiles asked Eddie Dixon, a bootblack, to approach fifteen-year-old Herbert Harris on lower Main Street and give him a note saying that Wiles was an emergency relief worker and had a job to offer him. He did, and the boy read the note and looked over Dixon's shoulder at Wiles, who stood beside a car he had borrowed. Harris walked up to Bob Wiles and after a few minutes of talking agreed to the job and got in the car. They drove off, passing J.M. Parker, a truck driver, who later testified with Dixon that he witnessed them driving out of town.

Wiles took the boy to an abandoned home twelve miles outside town. He confessed later that he took him to a room in the back of the house and sat talking to him for quite some time. Suddenly, something came over Wiles, and he picked up an iron bar and began beating the boy. He beat him down onto the ground and continued to strike him until he stopped moving. He dragged the young man's body to the corner of the room and covered him with an old mattress. Wiles drove back into town and, upon dropping the car off to his friend who had loaned it to him, passed Mr. Harris on the street. Wiles stuck out his hand, stopping Mr. Harris, and said cheerfully, "Merry Christmas." "Merry Christmas," Mr. Harris replied. And they proceeded on their way. By that afternoon, Mr. Harris and his wife were getting concerned. Hub had always been punctual, and the fact that he had not come home was odd. They raised the alarm, and the search was on. Green Griebner, whom Hub had been working for, was soon located, and he told of Hub leaving him to go and get another job. He described the man he went with and where he had been picked up. This tip led the police to speak with Dixon and Parker.

On Christmas Day, three men were driving along a back road outside of town when they decided that they needed to pull over and have another Christmas drink. They came to an abandoned house, and while two of the men tried to work the pump outside, another man went inside to check the house out. He saw blood and drag marks on the back porch leading into a room, where he could see the head of a body sticking out of a pile of cotton near an old mattress. Hub Harris had been found, and his parents could begin mourning their son. Meanwhile, the police had been led to Wiles, who made a confession after four and a half hours of questioning and after initially blaming two other men. The man who had once walked free from a double murder in Durham, North Carolina, found himself once more behind bars for taking a life. This time, though, there would be no trial and no reprieve.

"Good morning, gentlemen," Wiles said as he entered the small cold room where sat the electric chair. "Hello, Bill. Hello, Molly," he said to the guards as he walked past them. Slim and dressed in blue jeans and a prison shirt, head shaven, he shuffled to the chair and took his seat. He asked to speak to the prison chaplain, Reverend Phillips, as they strapped him in.

"Don't get it too tight," he said to one of the guards as he attached the electrode to his left leg. When they had completed their work, they stepped back, as did the reverend.

"Have any statement to make?" he was asked by the senior guard.

"Who is it I am talking to?" he asked as he looked around the room. "I'm guilty," he said, "I did it and am ready to pay for it. There was no one else in it at all." He went on to exonerate the two men he had falsely accused of helping him before going silent and just staring straight ahead. The guards came toward him to put the execution hood over his head and attach the electrode to his head. As they did, he spoke again in broken phrases, seeming to grasp verbally at some grand statement.

"Walk straight. You won't go wrong. I'm ready to pay...." His voice trailed off as they covered his face, and muffled words could still be heard by those

Cabin where the body of Herbert Harris was found. *From the* Columbia Record.

in the room. As the men took their positions and the executioner placed his hand on the switch, the muffled sounds became louder and clearer.

"Praise God from whom all blessings flow. Praise Him to all creatures here below," Wiles sang. "Praise God—." As the executioner flipped the switch, Wiles's body tensed and convulsed as if being thrown out of the chair against the straps. The switch was flipped back, and the body went limp. A second volt was shot through Bob Wiles, and his body again became animated and pulled at the straps. When the electricity was turned off the second time, the prison physician examined the body and pronounced him dead at 6:08 a.m. on March 12, 1934. Bob Wiles had promised the people of Durham when they set him free and made him a hero that he would prove to them that they made the right decision by the way he led his life. He had failed in that regard and brought more pain and suffering into the world for the Harris family and for his own.

ERNEST P. WALKER

The night of July 25, 1926, was warm and muggy, but it was cooler than it had been. Temperatures had reached triple digits days before, so the eighties seemed a lot more pleasant. Joseph Cassidy was sleeping soundly beside his wife, Lou, in their home on 1208 Fayetteville Street. Lou was restless and tossed and turned. She couldn't put her finger on why she could not sleep, but she lay listening to Joseph softly breathing beside her in the darkness.

On the street in front of the house, Ernest Walker staggered down the silent road, walking past the houses where families slept. An occasional dog would bark at him, but otherwise he walked alone. His wife had handed him a roll of cash that morning before leaving for work and told him to hold on to it for her to pay the bills. As soon as she left, he got dressed and headed out to drink. He had been drinking all day and night with his friends, and he was incredibly drunk.

Walker, as if driven by some dark force, stopped in front of the house where the Cassidys slept. Although very intoxicated, he was coming to the realization that he had spent all of the money his wife had given him and knew that he was going to have to hear about it when he got home. He made the decision to break into the house and steal any money he could. He crossed the street and went around the back of the house. Leaning against a tree was an axe, and he used it to cut the screen on the back window and pry it open. He climbed into the house and took the axe with him as he headed up the stairs.

Lou thought she heard something, but she wasn't sure. She sat up in bed and closed her eyes as if that would help enhance her hearing there in the darkness. "Joseph," she said quietly as she nudged her husband.

"What is it?" he asked sleepily.

"I heard something," she whispered. Joseph raised up slightly and listened.

"Must have been something at the neighbors' house," he said, laying his head back down and quickly falling back asleep. Lou listened intently for another few moments but heard nothing. Lying back down, she nuzzled down into the covers and into her pillow. Her senses were again alerted, though, by the creaking hinges of her bedroom door opening. She rolled over this time, less startled and more confused. In the doorway, with the ambient light from the street coming through the house, she could see the figure of a man holding what looked like a stick or a bat. She screamed!

Joseph sat up in bed, startled at his wife's scream, and the figure darted toward him, bringing the object down on his head. The blow glanced off, and Lou felt a mighty blow come down on her head simultaneously as blood from her husband splattered her. She touched her head and felt a large cut and blood oozing down her face. The figure raised what she now knew was an axe and brought it down on Joseph once more. As Lou rolled off the bed to flee, she heard a sickening thud behind her. She made for the door, but the assailant struck her twice in the back and side with the axe. She next felt herself being dragged into another room, where the intruder sexually assaulted her.

Walker stumbled back out of the room, through the house and back onto the street when he was done with his attack, escaping for the time being into the night. Lou crawled to the front door, and with what was left of her strength, she began to scream for help. Finally, lights began to come on around her, and neighbors came out of their house to find the source of the distress. When they found her, they rushed her and Joseph to Lincoln Hospital, where the latter died a few days later. Lou was in very critical condition for several days but lived.

Ernest Walker was soon caught. He lived only two blocks from the Cassidy home and was met face to face by his frantic wife when he got home that night. He was covered with blood on his coat, pants and shoes, and she would say later that he had a crazy look about him. In the next few days, his behavior around everyone led the police to his house to question him and search the home, where they found his bloody clothes in the closet. They were also able to get a confession from Walker. The police were able to lift his fingerprints from a buffet by the window where he broke in, and they were a match to Walker's prints.

He was charged with three capital crimes: burglary, murder and criminal assault. At the trial, the prosecutors submitted evidence that included the axe, the bloody clothes, the fingerprints and Walker's confession. The defense argued that Walker was mentally challenged, as well as drunk and insane at the time of the murder. They brought many people who knew him, and they testified that he was of very low intelligence and odd. The prosecutors rebutted this testimony by bringing in others who had worked with or employed Walker and testified that he was intellectually sharp. Lou Cassidy took the stand and testified about what she had seen that night and experienced. She testified that she could not see her attacker's face because of the darkness but that the figure that she saw matched the size of Walker. She also stated that during the sexual assault that she endured, she did not smell alcohol at all on her attacker.

Walker was found guilty in less than an hour of deliberation by the jury. The judge sentenced him to death in the electric chair. The time Ernest Walker spent in the state prison waiting for his death was quiet for him. He spoke little and rebuffed any attempts to speak to the prison's chaplain. On April 22, 1927, Ernest Walker was led through the prison to the cold octagon room where the electric chair sat waiting for him. He smiled as he entered the room but spoke little. The only coherent remarks recorded came as he walked past the police officers and detectives from Durham who had worked his case and took his confession. As he passed them, Walker turned to the prison chaplain, smiling, and said, "Them's my people," as if proud that they had come all of the way from Durham to see his end. Ernest Walker's wife had gone all the way to the governor to ask for a reprieve from the electric chair. She was under the impression that the execution would take up to three hours, and the thought of him in pain for that long was more than she could bear.

Her appeals were rejected, though, and at 10:36 a.m., they threw the switch. After the primary jolt, they ran another jolt through him to make sure he was gone. At 10:45 a.m., he was pronounced dead, and his body was carried out to the waiting gray hearse that sat in front of the prison. Ernest Walker paid the ultimate price for the wild night he had on the rent money his wife had entrusted to him. Many lives were ruined that night, and it is hard to assess if Ernest Walker had any remorse for anyone he hurt.

THE FIDELITY BANK ROBBERY

It was a typical Thursday at the Fidelity Bank in West Durham. Frank Upchurch, the bank manager, finished up some work at his desk and looked down at his watch. It was lunchtime. He stacked the papers that he was working on and tapped them on his desk to straighten them before locking them in the desk's drawer. Taking his hat from the coat rack by his door, he called over to his teller, C.C. Cole, and stenographer, Hazel Brown, that he was going to lunch and would be back soon. As he walked out of the bank into the August sunlight, he held the door for Mr. Erwin, one of the bank's customers, and headed down Ninth Street to find something to eat. He did not notice the blue Chevrolet parked near the bank or the three men who got out of the car and walked through the door behind Mr. Erwin.

One of the men stayed by the door, and the other two walked into the lobby. Cole looked up from his work and smiled at Mr. Erwin. His smile soon faded as he looked past him at the two men behind him who were pulling pistols from their coats. The man closest to Mr. Erwin shoved him forward and shouted as he pointed his pistol at Cole. "Throw 'em up or I'll shoot your heads off!"

Cole and Erwin immediately put their hands in the air. Hazel Brown stood up from her desk, and the other man pointed his pistol at her and motioned for her to go over with the others. They were led to the bank vault, and Cole was instructed to load all of the money into a sack. The gunman was calm and cool the entire time and gave orders clearly, as if this was not his first time. Cole and the others got a good look at the two men, both of

The old Fidelity Bank building is still standing today on Ninth Street. *Author's collection.*

whom were not wearing masks. One was short and stout, and the other was tall and skinny. They became aware that there was a third unseen man when the two began to converse with another man by the door while they were in the vault. Unbeknownst to them, Dr. D.S. Pepper from Duke Hospital, a regular customer, had come into the bank and was being brought back to the vault with the rest of them.

It seemed an eternity to the bank employees and customers, but the robbery lasted only a few minutes. After the money was loaded into a canvas sack, the four unfortunate hostages were closed in the bank vault, and the robbers made their getaway. First they drove the Chevy toward Hillsborough Road, but then they doubled back and were last seen passing Watts Hospital heading toward Guess Road. They had closed the vault but had not been aware of a safety mechanism that allowed someone trapped inside to free themselves. It took Cole about five minutes to get the vault open, and as they emerged, they found Frank Upchurch standing in the lobby holding his lunch and looking confused as to why the bank was completely empty.

The robbers had made a clean getaway. The blue Chevrolet was found later abandoned at the Rose of Sharon Church on Guess Road. The men who committed the crime had all been clearly seen and descriptions were given to the police, but no one recognized any of them. They had gotten away with $13,000, which included $7,000 that had been brought in that very morning for the Erwin Cotton Mill payroll that Friday. It was evident

The getaway car from the Fidelity Bank robbery was left in front of the Rose of Sharon Church in North Durham. *Author's collection.*

to all involved that the men had some inside knowledge of that fact and had been watching the bank and measured the optimal time to rob it—a time when the bank would be the least crowded and the manager would be gone.

They got a break just a few weeks later when the Carolina Bank and Trust Company in Denton, North Carolina, was robbed in a similar manner. Around lunchtime, three men entered the bank and demanded money from the teller. They got away with $6,000. Once again, they were seen heading in one direction and then doubled back. The car was found abandoned, just as it had been in the West Durham robbery. The main difference was the timing of the police response. Almost immediately, the High Point Police Department responded to the small town and set up a net and a very aggressive search for the perpetrators. There were several witnesses for the Denton robbery, and the police had good leads to go on. By the next day, they had four men in custody: Sylvan Palmer, Walter Bridgeman, Victor "Babyface" Fowler and Joe Horne. All of these men were known in the area as criminals. Palmer and Fowler were positively identified immediately by witnesses.

Fowler was already on bond for the shooting of railroad officer W.T. Butler. They were brought in and arrested. Horne and Bridgeman, who matched the description of the other two men but were not known by name, were sighted together by an officer. They were both under bond at the time for robbing the Kernersville Freight Station. The quick-acting officer tried to stop them, and they ran. He chased them down. Cutting through an alley, he was able to get ahead of the men and took them into custody.

While they were in jail waiting for trial, witnesses of the Fidelity bank robbery were brought to High Point to see if they could identify the men. Cole, Brown and Erwin positively identified Palmer as one of the robbers. Dr. Pepper could not confirm the identification of the men, although he said they were of similar size. When the men stood trial, there was a preponderance of evidence against them, including a large paper bag identified by a grocer who had sold Horne four apples earlier in the day of the robbery. The bag was also identified by the bank employees as being used in the robbery. It took the jury only three hours to convict the four men, landing them in jail for fifteen years. Over the next few years, a complicated web of confessions would cast doubt on the four men as they served their time.

In March 1935, Joe Horne was killed by another inmate in Duplin County. One month later, the three other men were pardoned. Three different men had confessed to the robbery in Denton in the preceding years, and the governor had taken that into consideration. Horne was pardoned posthumously for the crime. The robbery in Durham was never solved. Despite the identification of Palmer by the three witnesses in Durham, they felt that with the non-identification of Dr. Pepper, who was very well respected, they could not win a conviction.

MURDER OF DETECTIVE ROLAND GILL

Around 1:00 a.m. on June 10, 1933, the Durham Police Department received a call that the sound of breaking glass was heard coming from the Forlines Grocery Store on 1801 Erwin Road. Detectives Roland Gill, Jim Boyle and H.E. King responded to the call. When they got to the scene, they could clearly see that the bottom half of the glass of the front door was shattered. The three men gestured to one another their game plan: King would slip around the back to prevent the robber from escaping, if he was still in the building; Gill would stay out front and provide cover; and Boyle would enter the building to search for the burglar.

King disappeared around back, and Gill stood behind Boyle as he slipped through the hole in the broken glass. Boyle stood upright when he got through the door, and with his revolver in his right hand, he clicked on his flashlight with his left hand and began to sweep the store. He paced along the front of the store and shined his light down each aisle, illuminating cans of soup and other groceries. There was no sign of an intruder. He was about to head down the last aisle to check the back of the store when his light hit a man crouching behind a large can of lard in front of the meat counter. Boyle trained his gun on the man and ordered him to put his hands up and come out of his hiding spot. The man complied, and Boyle led him to the front of the store.

"I've got him right here," he called out to Gill, who shined his light on the two as they walked to the front of the store. Boyle noticed that the unbroken glass from the top of the door was sliding down, so he put his flashlight down and holstered his revolver. Gill carefully held the glass up while Boyle had the burglar crawl through. As he crawled across the broken glass, Boyle heard a noise coming from the back of the store.

"There's another one in there. Go get him," Roland told Boyle. He turned and moved back into the store to find the other burglar. He had no way of knowing that the noise had come from King, who was checking the backdoor to see if it was secure.

Roland Gill found himself momentarily alone with the suspect. As the burglar came to his feet on the other side of the door, he pulled a revolver out of his pocket and opened fire on Gill. He fired three times, hitting Roland in the mouth twice and once in the chest. Gill was still able to pull his revolver and return fire, although his shots were ineffective because of his severe injuries. The robber turned and ran through the night as King emerged from around the building and Boyle came back through the store, grabbing a large bag of flour and heaving it through the glass door.

King got close enough to the gunman to have his left eye burned by powder, and he and Boyle emptied their revolvers at the man as he fled into the night. King, though near blind, gave chase through the dark alleys of the nearby houses and buildings. Boyle stayed with Gill, who collapsed after firing at the man. Boyle rushed him in the car to Duke Hospital, where he died at 1:28 a.m. King was unable to find his man, but he did manage to find the hat that he was wearing and a partial blood trail. It would prove to be a good starting point.

A posse was formed to hunt the killer down, and bloodhounds were brought in. A large group of lawmen and citizens set out in different directions looking for the fugitive. Detectives E.R. Leary and M.M. Thompson soon picked up his trail about a half mile from the place King had found the hat and blood. When they caught up with him, they fired at him but missed. Given the way he was running, they could tell he was wounded already, and they finally caught up with him hiding in a thicket of honeysuckles. He had been shot several times in the stomach and still had the gun he had killed Gill with on him. He told the detectives that his name was John Reade.

As they walked him back to the scene, they came upon more and more men from the posse who were uninterested in taking "John Reade" back to stand trial. Their job quickly changed from finding the man to protecting him so that he might face justice. They got him through the crowd and took him to Lincoln Hospital, where the doctors told them that he had little chance of survival. Despite this, they propped him up in bed, fingerprinted him and took his picture. While he lay dying in the hospital, they were able to identify him as Jesse Brooks of South Carolina, a man who was no stranger to the law and was wanted in several states from Maryland to Georgia.

Brooks served time in Georgia in 1921 and later in Virginia under an alias. It was believed that he had murdered at least two people and had committed a rape in Baltimore, Maryland. The Durham Police Department mourned its loss as Brooks fought for his life in the hospital. At the funeral for Roland Gill, the sorrowful minister looked out at the crowd gathered to say goodbye. "There is no need for me to recite the circumstances of his death. To say that he died in the line of duty is sufficient," he spoke. "Our Father, give protection to his fellow officers as they go about their work." A solemn "Amen" reverberated throughout the crowd and subsided to silence once more, broken only by the sobs of Roland Gill's widow.

At Lincoln Hospital, a medical miracle was taking place, although few would be rejoicing for the once dying Jesse Brooks. Doctors marveled as his vital signs steadily improved and he stabilized. They soon reported to the police that he was going to make it somehow. He would live at least until the judicial system had its say. This turnaround led to another problem for the authorities, as a vengeful crowd gathered outside the hospital, with talk of lynching becoming common among the restless group. To avoid that, Sheriff Belvin, along with four of his most trusted deputies—Lonnie Morgan, J.E. Ferrell, Norman Shaw and Onus Hall—snuck Brooks out of the hospital in the dead of the night and slipped through the crowd. He was taken to Central Prison in Raleigh, where he finished his recovery before his trial.

Before the end of June, he was indicted for the murder of Roland Gill, and on July 19, 1933, he was convicted after only thirty minutes of deliberation. He was sentenced to be electrocuted on September 15, but he was saved by his appeal. The case went before the North Carolina Supreme Court in February 1934, but the judges found no error in the ruling. On March 16 of that year, he entered the execution chamber at Central Prison with a smile on his face. He had found peace in Christianity after a life of crime, and he greeted the witnesses one by one as he passed them by. As he sat, hooked up and head covered with a hood, waiting the power of the electric chair to course through his body, he could be heard saying, "Praise the Lord, praise the Lord, praise the Lord." At 10:32 a.m., he was pronounced dead.

Before his death, Brooks had written out a lengthy confession. His words did little to soothe the hurt he had caused:

> *I am very sorry but God is truth, so I must now make a clean confession of all the crimes in which I have done, for in the Bible we are told to make a*

clean breast. Confession is good for the soul, and I want to not let anything keep me, Jesse Brooks, out of the Kingdom of God who loved the world that he gave his only son for the sins of the world. Now we start.

The first crime that I committed was in a little town in Abbyville, South Carolina. It was a store robbing. I was hired by a man to look after his little children. When I went in I took from his cash register 25 cents. As I did not get caught, I ventured on. Then I quit my job and started out in a big way. I left there and went to Georgia and tried two or three store robberies. Some of these were where people were sleeping, but slipping along like a cat after a mouse, I did not wake them up, so I got some money and jewelry and other valuables which I sold and that gave me plenty of nerve. Then I came back to my home in Abbeyville where my dear sister Janie was at the point of death. My brother and I got into a fuss and I got a pistol and shot him dead. Then I had to leave but I heard my sister died in twenty-four hours after I left.

From my time of crime and disobedience has caused the death of my mother, father, three sisters and brother. I am sorry but I don't know where any of my loved ones are buried. Well, after I shot my brother, I went back to Georgia where I met a girl where I planned one of my robberies and she refused my demand and the only thing I knew to do was to draw my gun and shoot her through the mouth. That crime forced me to leave again. Then I went to Portsmouth, charged with a midnight robbery and given seven years. I pulled that time in Richmond. Left there and went back down through the state, was caught in South Carolina and given four years. I beat this rap by leaving the guard standing and looking at me run. I was never caught so that gave me some encouragement. I have always been a man who went by myself and have pulled some robberies alone and other crimes I committed against my fellow man. I have done everything in my history of crime, I have broken every law of the land, and also every commandment of the Bible. I ask you not to try to do as I have done or you will sure get caught. And the last thing I done was robbery on the night of June 9, about 1:30 and got $2 in this. I got shot myself but later got caught on account of loss of blood. The same night about 2:30 I killed a man named Roland Gill and was tried by Hon. court, N.C. The sentence was to be electrocuted for this crime. I want to thank all the good people and attorneys that fought for me. Not his fault, no one else but mine. I am to blame for all. May God bless each of you now, and ever more. I want to thank all the good people who give their time to God and I feel it my duty to quote Matthew 25:42 verse to 46

A vacant lot is all that remains where Forelines Grocery Store once stood. This is where Detective Roland Gill was killed responding to a robbery. *Author's collection.*

verses, Christ has washed my sins as white as snow for I know in the day of judgement we shall all stand before the throne of God and I know I will be there. Stop, stop, sinners, you all have to die!

Those present included King, Boyle, Captain W.E. Burgess, M.M. Thompson, W.L. Seabock and Roland's brother, Jerdie Gill. It was against the rules of the prison for a member of the family to be present at an execution, but someone at the prison had let him slip in. Gill's wife and young son were outside, parked on the street. When the press spoke to Mrs. Gill, she was unapologetic in her feelings: "That man's death has done more good than anything in the world. Why, I feel a thousand times better since he was killed. I think his execution was a good thing. In the first place, no punishment was bad enough for him, but I think his execution will help teach people that they can't break the law and get away with it." Whether it taught that lesson to anyone other than Jesse Brooks is up for debate. But it certainly ended a life of crime and gave comfort to a distraught widow.

THE COURIER ROBBERY

On August 16, 1935, R.D. "Dee" Herndon walked out of the Durham branch of the Fidelity bank in Durham and got into the waiting sedan driven by his wife. She often picked him up from work and drove him to the Bank of Chapel Hill to make the bank's deposit. R.D. enjoyed her company and leaned over for a kiss as he threw the black leather bag into the back seat. She coldly presented her cheek to him without acknowledging him in any other way. It was typical, and he didn't really mind. It was just her way, he told himself as they drove off. He tried to make small talk, but Mrs. Herndon was just not in the mood. He soon found himself just looking out of the window at the plush green scenery they passed. The silence of the ride was finally broken as they passed over New Hope Creek.

"Dear," she said, "I think this car is trying to get us to stop." He looked over his shoulder and was startled at how close the car was to theirs. The faces of the men in the car were clear, and he thought there couldn't have been enough space in between the vehicles to put a sheet of paper. Before he could speak, the car whipped around them and came up along side. The passenger pulled out a pistol and pointed it at them.

"Pull over!" the man screamed, and Mrs. Herndon complied. The two men jumped from the car and held the Herndons at gunpoint. They went straight to the black leather bag in the backseat and told them that if they tried anything or even looked at them, they would be killed. Mr. and Mrs. Herndon complied. Soon, one of the men ran to the front of the car and opened the hood. They could see him jerking at the wires trying to disable the car. He jumped in their black coupe, and they drove off. The robbers made off with $10,525 in cash and coins. R.D. bounded out of the car and was under the hood himself in seconds trying to get the car started. A World War I veteran, he was keen to catch up to the robbers and see if he could retrieve the money. It had killed him to sit and let them take the money, but he felt like he had to do whatever they asked to make sure that his wife was safe. He soon got back on to the road and headed toward Chapel Hill. Realizing that he had lost his chance to catch up to them, he pulled into a service station, but they did not have a working phone for him to use. So, he drove on to the Bank of Chapel Hill, where he reported the robbery.

The police went to work to find the men responsible for the robbery. The only clue they had was that the men looked to be in their mid-twenties. It didn't take long for them men to show themselves, as the next night, the bandits gathered at Thompson's filling station on Wake Forest Highway. The group of men was led by Claude Herndon, a second cousin of R.D., who freely spent money and bought drinks for everyone and spoke openly of the robbery. He was soon arrested, and so were three other men who had participated in the robbery—Richard Chamberlin, whom the police accused of planning the robbery; Worth Vaughan, who was the driver; and Lewis Rigsbee, who was the gunman. R.D. easily identified the two men who had been present, but he was soon surprised at the story they told to the police.

All of the men arrested for the robbery told the police that they had been propositioned to do the robbery at the behest of Mrs. Herndon herself. Claude testified that Mrs. Herndon had come to his house and told him that it would be like "taking candy from a baby" to get the payroll. Claude's neighbors testified that she had indeed visited his house on many occasions without her husband. Claude said that he reached out to Chamberlin because he knew that he could get a crew together to execute the robbery. All of the men were offered between $300 and $500 for their part in the robbery. Lewis Rigsbee testified that on the day of the robbery, Mrs. Herndon waved a handkerchief out of the window when her husband got in the car to signal that he had the payroll. She was soon arrested and found herself on trial.

Middle-aged and motherly, Mrs. Herndon seemed out of place in the courtroom. Witness after witness took the stand. Her coconspirators also took the stand and laid out the plot. They testified that they had tried before, but she had not given the signal, and she swore to them that she would not identify them if they were caught. Many people testified that she was a woman of great character. The testimony that possibly put the nail in her coffin was that of a coworker of Claude's. He was a bus driver for the City of Durham and testified that she had come by the bus station a few days before the robbery and asked for Claude. He was not there, and the bus driver told her that. She asked him to give Claude a message saying that what they had agreed on before still stood and that she had confidence in him. The prosecutor argued that Mrs. Herndon wanted the money because of her advancing age and the fact that R.D. was in bad health and could not acquire any life insurance that would take care of her after he passed.

Her attorney, Walter Siler, gave a passionate and entertaining defense of Mrs. Herndon with his closing argument. A small man with sandy blond hair, he was described even at the time as an old-school attorney. He stood before the jury and delivered his speech in the most bellicose manner possible.

"This is an extraordinary case. None of you has ever beheld a case like this. You are asked to go into one of the most respectable homes in North Carolina and brand a woman as a felon upon the testimony of a gang of thugs, thieves, and highwaymen."

"And Chamberlain!" he shouted. "Isn't he a sweet-smelling geranium? Why he'd poison a whole Sunday school at a picnic for 15 cents just to keep in practice….I tell you gentlemen if you convict this woman on the testimony of these skunks we may as well blot out the star in our flag which represents North Carolina, but leave the stripe as a fitting symbol of our degradation….Not only do these perjured lips seek to swear away the liberty of this woman but also to destroy her character."

He continued, "They even go as far as to attempt to destroy her character by saying she went to a picture show with Claude Herndon. What if she did? Since when did Durham become such a Sodom that women lost their character when they went to a movie? I say if Claude Herndon's veiled implications are true and none of us believe them, but I say if it is true that his friendship for her was more than platonic then he is a skunk to tell of it now, and if it is untrue, he is just as bad. The state would have you take that skunk to your bosom and send a woman of good character to the penitentiary."

Siler hooked his hands in his suspenders and walked with chest puffed out in front of the jury. Gazing into each of the men's eyes, he continued, "Why, gentleman, if you set a precedent by doing this then none of us will be safe. Any highwayman might get up in court and accuse you of being in on a crime. Claude Herndon might have implicated the bank cashier had he been so minded and all of us know that there is no suggestions that he had anything to do with the robbery."

He stopped, unhooked his fingers from their resting place on his suspenders and began to bring his right hand down into his open left hand as he spoke, giving the jury the sense of his laying out the truth for them to consume. "I'll tell you what they did, they saw that Bozo got $300 of the stolen money for implicating them and they said among themselves, 'If he gets $300 and freedom for implicating a bunch of highwaymen, then what might we get if we involve some person of good character?'"

The courtroom was moved to laughter on many occasions as he finished his deep-throated defense of his client, but when the show was over, it was time for the jury to deliberate. They found her guilty of larceny, and the judge sentenced her to eight years in prison. As the sentence was read, her husband, who had stood beside her the entire time, put his arm around her and consoled her. She would only serve three years, being paroled later for good behavior. Dee passed away in 1941 at the age of fifty-four.

THE WICKED DEED OF ED ALSTON

Christmas Eve 1937 was a dreary, rainy and overcast all day. It was the perfect day for a nap. Janie Wilkerson, 103-year-old grandmother, was thinking that very thing as she lay across the bed in the room she was renting on Piedmont Avenue. Her granddaughter, nineteen-year-old Frances Elliot, was there with her. Frances loved her grandmother very much and was looking forward to spending Christmas Day with her. There were always people in and out of the house, and it seemed to Frances that she shared her grandmother with the community of Hayti in northern Durham. Earlier, her cousin Richard had come by and given Janie some money to hold for him. Ed Alston, a tobacco worker who rented a room from Janie, was somewhere around the house, as was a neighborhood boy named Charles Ansley. As the rain beat against her window, Frances slipped into sleep in the front room of the house. In the back room, Janie Wilkerson lay across her bed sleeping.

Sometime that afternoon, as Charles Ansley sat in a chair watching the rain fall, Ed Alston appeared behind him. "Let's go boy," he said as he took Charles by the arm and led him to the door.

"Why do I got to leave?" Charles asked as Alston opened the door and pushed him out into the rain with no explanation. Dejected, Charles ran down the alley to his own house on Enterprise Street and sat on the porch to dry off before going inside.

Back at the Janie Wilkerson's house, Ed Alston closed the door and walked to the kitchen. He took a piece of firewood from the stove and walked to the back bedroom where Ms. Wilkerson slept. He stood over her and gazed at her softly breathing. Suddenly, Alston raised the firewood over his head and swung it down on Janie. Again and again, he brought the wood down on her as blood splattered across the room. When he was done, he threw the wood down on the floor and began to rifle through her clothing. Inside her dress he found a woven bag sewed to a string that he tore out and looked inside. Just as he thought: it was the money he had seen Richard bring her earlier for her to keep.

As Alston looked at the money purse, he heard movement in the front room. Frances may have heard him. He stuck the money in his pocket and picked the firewood up again. He moved into the hall, creeping along the wall toward the room where Frances had been sleeping. He came to the door and pushed it open. Frances was sitting up on the bed from her nap and barely caught the sight of Ed Alston as he flung himself on her and hit her with the stick of wood. After a few strikes, Alston again discarded the wood and fled the house. A still wet Charles Ansley saw Ed Alston run from the alley and down Enterprise Street away from the house.

It wasn't long before the ladies were found and taken to Duke Hospital, where Janie soon died. The Durham Police Department set about investigating the murder of Janie and the brutal beating of Frances, who was still in critical condition in the hospital. They found several witnesses, including Charles, who said that they saw Ed Alston fleeing the home around the time of the attack. Alston was a tobacco worker and was known around the neighborhood, although no one would have believed that he was capable of the murder. Most of the people who knew him were surprised by the brutal crimes. He was arrested shortly after the witnesses came forward and confessed to the crime almost immediately.

He said that he had seen his friend Richard Holman give his grandmother Janie Wilkerson sixty dollars earlier that day to hold for him. He had entered Janie's bedroom planning to steal the money from her. He told the police that he hit her only once, but the brutal scene told a different story. He also admitted to hitting Frances for fear that she had heard something and would tell on him. Alston told the police that he drank an entire pint of whiskey just prior to the attack and had started on another one. He admitted to taking twelve dollars from the house when he fled.

Alston was prosecuted by solicitor Leo Carr and defended by Sigmund Meyer and C.W. Hall. Judge W.H. Burgwin presided over the trial, which was contentious and close. The defense argued that Alston was intoxicated at the time of the attack and had attempted to commit burglary. He attacked in the heat of the moment while committing the lesser crime, and they pleaded for a second-degree murder conviction instead of a first-degree murder. This would put their client in jail for many years, maybe even for life, but it would spare him the gas chamber.

The prosecution argued that Alston may have been intoxicated, but people are intoxicated all of the time and do not commit brutal crimes such as this. Also, they pointed out that it was not just a matter of a single blow to "keep them from crying out." It had been a devastating beating that had killed Janie and put Frances in the hospital for many weeks. When the jury first convened, they were deadlocked at six votes to six. After fifteen hours of deliberation, after 10:00 p.m. on a Thursday night, they came to a verdict.

On February 19, 1938, Judge Burgwin read the verdict to a packed courtroom: guilty. A murmur went through the room as both those who thought the verdict was just celebrated and those who had hoped the young man's life would be spared complained. Ed Alston sat beside his lawyers, stone faced and emotionless as he had throughout the trial.

After more than a year of appeals, retrials and extensions, Ed Alston finally faced justice in the gas chamber at Central Prison in Raleigh. He claimed that the confession he signed was false and that he was afraid when speaking with the police after he was arrested. But the evidence was overwhelming against him. They led him stoically into the chamber that summer morning to meet his fate, but before the lever was pulled and the gas released, he was asked if he had anything to say. "I did it, and I want you all to forgive me. I am the one," he said solemnly.

The prison chaplain, L.A. Watts, asked him if he was saved, and he said yes. At 10:02 a.m. on June 16, 1939, the gas was released into the chamber. Thirteen minutes later, Ed Alston was dead.

THE HALL BROTHERS OF DURHAM

On the steaming night of July 15, 1939, a call came into the Durham County Sheriff's Department of a domestic disturbance on Fayetteville Road right outside the city limits. It was about nine o'clock when the call came in that James Smith was threatening his family and neighbors with a shotgun and that they needed someone to come out and get him. Deputy Onus Hall, known as a good deputy and a good man, answered the call. He had with him Deputy J.E. Ferrell and highway patrolman R.H. Sutton, who had been at the station when the call came in and decided to tag along. They drove off into the night for what seemed to be a very routine call.

When they arrived, everything seemed quiet and calm. No one was around up and down the street as Deputy Hall stepped out of the car. Patrolman Sutton got out of the car on the other side and looked around for the disturbance. Suddenly, Smith stepped out from a row of hedges in front of the house with a shotgun. Sutton saw him rise and raise the shotgun in the direction of Hall, but he was too late to stop him. Sutton pulled his revolver and emptied it into Smith, who collapsed back into the bushes dead. Ferrell and Sutton pulled Hall into the car and sped as fast as they could to Watts Hospital on Broad Street. The doctors and nurses worked feverishly to save him, but he soon passed away. The gaping wound that he had suffered was just too much for his body to take.

Memorial services were held for Onus Hall. A peace-loving man who always sought to find the best solution to any problem before things escalated, he was also known as a brave man who never shirked his duty. His death was also a grim reminder of another deputy who was killed ten years earlier in Durham. The similarities of the two slayings were stark. Both deputies were ambushed and killed without a chance to defend themselves. Ten years earlier, the deputy who was killed was Will E. Hall, the brother of Onus.

In October 1929, Deputy Sheriff Will Hall, along with Deputy (and future sheriff) Eugene "Cat" Belvin, set out toward Pearsontown in southern Durham hunting for a liquor still. Hall was known as an intrepid and popular deputy in Durham and seemed to know everyone. They parked their car on a dirt road and looked into the tangled woods where they had been told the still was. The two deputies decided to split up to cover more ground and meet back at the car to tell each other what they had found. Hall went left, while Belvin went right, a coinflip decision that would affect the history of policing in Durham for a generation.

When Deputy Belvin returned to the car, Hall was nowhere to be found. Belvin called out for him, and when he did not receive an answer, he headed into the woods, taking the path that Hall had taken. As he pushed through deeper into the foliage, following the steps he felt his partner would have taken, he began to play out in his mind all of the reasons for his delay. Had he gotten lost? Had he found the still and was destroying it? Had he found the bootleggers and made arrests? Was Hall somewhere ahead of him waiting for backup? All of these questions ran through his mind as he crawled over downed trees and went up and down gullies. It was on the downward slope of one of these gullies that he saw the prone body of Will Hall, face first in the leaves with a devastating wound in his back.

Belvin pulled his pistol from his pocket and crouched down. There was no need to rush because it was obvious from his vantage point that Hall was dead. Belvin was not called "Cat" for no reason, and he scanned the area for the killer or killers before he made a move toward the body. Finally, he crept forward and looked down on the man whom he had known as fearless and tough. There was a four-inch-diameter wound on his back toward the left side. It was apparent that Hall was in the process of turning around when he was shot. Belvin thought that he must have heard whoever was behind him just a second too late. Belvin thought what a lucky bastard that must have been because had he given Will Hall just a moment more, his partner would have been the one who came out on top in that gunfight. It was only through an act of cowardice that the murderer had walked away on two feet.

Belvin marked his trail as he went back for help, and when they came to collect Hall's body, they found a fifteen-gallon whiskey cache just a few more yards from him in the woods. Hall had stumbled on the bootleg liquor that was waiting for transport to its final destination and obviously aroused

Sheriff Eugene "Cat" Belvin served Durham County as a deputy and later sheriff for more than fifty years. *From the Durham Sun.*

the person who had been left to guard the stash. Sheriff John Harward made the investigation the priority of the department, and soon they found their man.

John and Rose Belle Gilchrist reported that Nathan Blake, who rented a room from them, had borrowed John's shotgun that morning saying that he wanted to go squirrel hunting. When he came home, he was distressed and said that he had lost the gun. When the sheriff questioned him, he quickly confessed. He told them that he had been hired by rumrunners to guard the cache at the transport point and needed a gun. He had borrowed the shotgun and took his post with the whiskey. He was surprised by the deputy when he came creeping through the woods right toward him. Blake said he was so scared and pushed himself back up into the ground on the slope of the hill he sat on. Hall walked right past him so close that Blake thought for sure he was caught. When Hall passed him, he felt a monetary relief, but then he stopped and began to turn toward him. Blake told the sheriff that it was then that he panicked and shot Hall in the back. Blake told them that he had been told by the rumrunners to kill anyone who came near the stash.

The trial was quick and without much controversy. He was convicted of first-degree murder and sentenced to death. A new lawyer took Blake's case, though, and appealed on the grounds that he said Blake had not been allowed to testify for himself at the first trial and that the confession was coerced. In the second trial, he pleaded guilty to second-degree murder and was sentenced to thirty years in prison. The legal maneuvering of his attorney had saved his life. He would go on to escape from a prison camp in Rolesville, North Carolina, only to be rearrested just a few days later. Then he would die in prison of natural causes in 1941.

Sheriff Harward had to replace Deputy Will Hall, and he soon found his man. Onus Hall, his brother, stepped up to take on the role, not knowing that a decade later, he would be the victim of a similar murder. The Hall family was not done making an impact on the Durham County Sheriff's Office. In 1955, Levester Hall, the son of Onus and the nephew of Will, was sworn in as a deputy and would serve with distinction for many years.

ARTHUR "LUCKY" MORRIS

In the summer of 1939, Governor Clyde Hoey had a big decision to make. A man of contrasting morals, he held the life of a young man in his hands. Arthur Morris was twenty-three years old, sitting on death row and awaiting his fate for the crime of burglary, which was a capital crime in North Carolina. Hoey was a staunch segregationist and had prosecuted the murderer of Gastonia Police Chief Orville Aderholt, who was killed during the Loray Mill strike in 1929. He was quoted in a speech to the United Daughters of the Confederacy: "Niggers are not entitled to civil rights and will never get them. There were no niggers on the Mayflower." Yet he had appointed the first Black man to be a trustee for Black colleges and had fought for funding for higher education for African Americans—segregated of course, but funding nonetheless. Although his sense of racial justice was lacking and his feelings toward Black North Carolinians was unfavorable, he did have a sense of trepidation at putting a young man to death for the crime of burglary. Robbing a house that was unoccupied was not a capital crime. It was the act of robbing the house while it was occupied that made it so. Hoey stepped in at the eleventh hour to grant a short reprieve to deliberate a possible commutation and save his life. A few days later, he released a six-and-a-half-page paper detailing his decision. Morris would indeed keep his date with the executioner.

Arthur Morris had many nicknames by the time he sat on death row, including "Lucky," "The Eel" and "The Grey Mouse." His picture in the papers showed a baby-faced young man, but he had, in fact, accumulated a record that Hoey said was "probably unmatched in the history of criminal justice in the state." He had begun his life of crime in 1932, when he was convicted of carrying a concealed weapon and breaking and entering in New Jersey. Because he was a youth at the time, he was sent to a reformatory in Rahway, New Jersey, and was taught a trade. When he left the reformatory, he headed south to Durham, where he went to work burglarizing houses. By the time he was arrested, he had been indicted for eight capital charges, all for burglary. Although no one was killed during these crimes, there were large sums of money that had been taken, and there had been at least two cases where there were reports of attempted sexual violence and assault.

In December 1937, a girl stated that she was awakened by a man molesting her under the sheets of her bed. She screamed, and the man shined a flashlight into her face. She covered her eyes, and when the light was turned off, she saw the shape of a man fleeing her room. She testified only to the man's stature, but her jewelry was found on Morris when he was arrested. In another similar case, a woman was awakened by a flashlight shining in her face. She was paralyzed with fear, and the man began to touch her legs and her private parts under the sheets. She pleaded with him to stop, but he continued. When she screamed, he stood up, struck her in the head with the flashlight and fled. She fought him off despite her head injury, and he fled. Again she could only testify to his stature because of the darkness, but he was found to have a ring that was stolen in his possession when he was caught.

Morris pleaded guilty to lesser charges than burglary in an attempt to save his life. He admitted to having taken a pistol into the house he robbed and stated that he had it in case he found himself in a situation where he was caught in a house. When he was arrested in Durham, he had suits of clothing, watches, rings, bracelets and other jewelry that many of his victims were able to claim. The Durham Police Department suspected him of many more burglaries because there were many items that were never claimed. He was sentenced to fifty to eighty years and was sent away to prison. But on June 10, 1938, he and another inmate escaped from a Perquimans County Prison road crew with two other inmates. The others were caught shortly after their escape, but Morris was able to elude the police for three weeks, during which time he went right back to his life of crime. A string of burglaries and robberies in Henderson led the local police to suspect that he was in the area. When he left his hat in the home of one of his victims, they were sure that he was in the area. Henderson Police Chief J.H. Langston and his officers surrounded a motel on a tip and found him in a room surrounded by stolen items. They arrested him, and after deliberating with law enforcement in Durham and Wake County, they decided to send him to Central Prison while Wake County prepared a case from the previous December for capital burglary.

By the time he was arrested in Henderson, the authorities who had allowed him to plead guilty to lesser charges had lost their inclination for leniency. Morris soon found himself on trial again for the burglary of Dr. William Dewar of Raleigh. The doctor had been awakened by the figure of a man in his house rifling through his belongings. He had stayed in bed and stayed quiet for fear of inciting a confrontation and watched as the man took several items and then left his house with twenty cents and a check for eighty dollars. Arthur Morris, the day after the burglary, walked into a Durham bank and tried to cash the check made out to Dr. William Dewar. The suspicious teller had told him that he would have to come back later, and when he did, two Durham police officers were waiting for him. It had been the last crime he had committed before being imprisoned, and he was allowed to plead to lesser charges. He had not been tried for the crime since he had been allowed the plea deal, and it showed that he had been in a house while it was occupied. Morris was easily convicted of capital burglary and sentenced to death.

Governor Hoey had taken in all of the information he had on the young man. After looking at the totality and the escalating nature of the crimes, he decided that he would not allow Morris a reprieve. Hoey stated, "If I had to deal with only one case, and that case of the burglary of Dr. Dewar's house, it would be easy to commute this sentence, but as I stated at the outset, I am dealing here with a man who could easily have been convicted of a dozen or so other cases, some of them involving violence." It was thought that he had committed up to fifty burglaries and countless robberies of homes. Many cases of burglaries that had involved violence and attempted sexual assault were never attributed to Morris, but could not be ruled out either. Hoey felt that it was just a matter of time before Morris would take the crime to the limit and commit a more heinous crime—a crime he felt that he could not bear to have on his conscience.

"If Morris was a man of different amenable nature, if he were amenable to discipline, it would not have been necessary for the state to place him on trial for his life. However, the determined manner in which this man has returned again and again to the commission of capital felonies has made it necessary for the state to take such action as will, under the law, give it complete protection."

Arthur Morris was executed on September 1, 1939. He walked smiling to the gas chamber while fellow inmates sang "What a Friend I Have in Jesus." He shook hands with the guards and the executioner. The warden helped strap him into the chair, and they exited the room. Morris waved his hand at the witnesses and took a deep breath as the gas entered the chamber. Before two minutes had passed, he fell unconscious. It took fifteen minutes for Morris to pass. His death would later be used in arguments against the death penalty as a mandatory punishment for burglary. In North Carolina, it would take until 1977, after several Supreme Court rulings and criminal justice reform, for burglary to be removed from classification as a capital crime.

ROSANA AND DANIEL PHILLIPS

Rosana Phillips sat in a holding cell watching the clock on the wall tick. She was nervous and scared, but deep down she just knew that fortune would shine on her at any moment. Even if her husband, Danny, did not confess to the crime they had been convicted of before his execution, she was sure that the governor would not allow a woman to be executed. She was wrong.

At 10:58 a.m., she was led into the chamber where moments before her husband, Daniel Phillips, had died. He did not take responsibility for the crime as she had hoped. He offered only a goodbye to his cellmates on death row and said that he was "ready to die," that he hoped to "see them in Heaven." The warden of the prison hoped that in his last statement he would give some confession exonerating Rosana. He did not like the idea of executing a woman, but the law was the law; with the lack of additional information, he had no choice. It took Daniel twelve minutes to die. He was taken away, and the chamber was readied for her.

She had come to the gas chamber after a hard life. Born to a young, unwed mother who was unable to provide her with a stable home, she was raised by her grandmother for the first six years of her life. Once her grandmother died, her mother came back into her life. Rosana found herself for the most part fending for herself and without a positive role model, and it was early on in her childhood that she began committing small crimes and being sexually promiscuous. She became pregnant at the age of fourteen and dropped out of school.

By seventeen, she was in big trouble. She was arrested on charges of public drunkenness and assault on a police officer and received a sentence of two years in prison. It was when she left prison that she first met the farmer and millworker Daniel Phillips and began a relationship with him.

It was a tumultuous and sometimes violent relationship. They constantly fought and would be at each other's throats one minute but then back together soon after. Rosana had another child who was not Daniel's, but he took her back. By 1942, they had gone to work as sharecroppers and housekeepers for Harry F. Watkins, a Durham farmer.

In September, a neighbor of Mr. Watkins was getting water from a well on his property when he made a grisly discovery. At the bottom of the well was a decomposing corpse. The body was recovered and identified as Harry Watkins. He had been struck on the back of the head with a devastating blow from what appeared to be an axe and another blow on the front of the body at the base of the neck, almost severing the head.

Police immediately looked for the Phillipses to question them but found that they had fled. They were tracked down and arrested in South Carolina, where they had gotten married and were honeymooning comfortably on a large amount of money. Rosana had bought a new hat and a blue, two-piece gingham short playsuit. Their honeymoon came to an abrupt end, as they were taken back to Durham to stand trial.

It was soon after they were taken into custody that they turned on each other, both pointing the finger of blame squarely at the other. Daniel said that Mr. Watkins had begun to argue with Rosana and that as he turned his back to walk away, Rosana struck a blow on the back of his head with an axe. She had made him drag the body out to their car and had also forced him to also hit the body with the axe. He had not wanted to, but she had insisted; he struck the dead body on the neck with the axe before he helped her put the body in the car. Daniel claimed that she had gone to South Carolina to see a "root doctor" and had put a voodoo spell on him that forced him to do as she said and to marry her.

Rosana had a much different story. She claimed that she had been washing dishes and looking out of the small window above the sink when she saw Daniel talking to Mr. Watkins in the yard. Watkins had turned around and was walking away when Daniel struck him in the back of the head with an axe and then again after he fell. He dragged the body to the car and then came inside and made her come help him lift the body into the car and dump it in the well, where the body had been found.

Her story was much more believable, but to the jury, it was evident that both were culpable no matter which story was true. Even if Rosana had not struck a blow, she had helped him dump the body and had run away with Daniel. She had married him and was spending the money that had been taken from Mr. Watkins, so they found little sympathy for her. It was a thirteen-hour trial and a unanimous decision that they would both be put to death.

No woman had been put to death in North Carolina since 1910, and although she had been very nervous, it was not until the prison's matron came for her that Rosana really believed they would execute her. As they strapped her into the chair in the gas chamber, she knew there was no longer any hope. They closed the door, and she heard the switch being flipped to activate the trapdoor dropping the hydrocyanide balls into the sulfuric acid solution to create the toxic gas. She waited, breathing heavy and scared, but nothing happened. She could see the men working the levers outside of the chamber and knew that something was wrong. Soon, the door was opened again, and she was told that the trapdoor had become stuck. They would have to do it again.

They adjusted the door, and the process started again. This time, when they flipped the lever, she found herself choking and gasping for air. She died at 11:08 a.m. on New Year's Day 1943. Reverend L. Watts told the press that he had spoken with both of them before the execution and that they had forgiven each other. With that, their toxic relationship had come to a deadly end.

DEATH OF A LIQUOR KINGPIN

In the early morning hours of December 22, 1943, Willie Green, a tenant farmer, walked along a dirt road that cut through woods and tobacco fields near Patterson Township on the outskirts of Durham. The air was crisp and cold, and silence swallowed him as he walked along. In the distance, he could vaguely see a glimmer of a light. His steps quickened as he moved toward what began to materialize as a car on the side of the road. Willie felt a high level of anxiety as to what he could face ahead as he walked. "No one should be out this time of night, even myself," he thought. As he came abreast to the car, he could see that it was a red Buick sedan that was pulled off the road at an angle with its lights on. He could see that the trunk was open, but he tried to keep his eyes focused on what was in front of him. Silence remained around him as he walked past the car and could not see another living soul. "None of my business," he thought as he hurried by and headed for home.

When he arrived home, the odd scene was still on his mind. Willie stopped on the front porch of his modest cabin and prepared himself for the wrath his wife was going to have for him for coming in so late. His fears were dissuaded, though, when he came into a quiet house and could hear her gently snoring from the bed in the corner. Willie silently slipped off his shoes and snuggled into the warm bed, thankful to be home. After a brief skirmish in the morning with the missus, what he had seen the night before was still on his mind. He knew that curiosity killed the cat, but he felt compelled to

Illustration of the murder of liquor kingpin Logan Forsyth. *From the* Durham Sun.

go back and see if the car was still there or if there was any evidence of what had been going on in the darkness of the morning. He set off back down the road that had brought him home the morning before. As he drew closer to the car he had seen the morning before, the scene was becoming clearer to him. He saw the dim lights of the car still on and the body of a man in blue denim overalls face down in the ditch next to the car. His body had been hidden by the car and darkness hours before. A ten-dollar bill lay crumpled in the road in front of the car. He probably walked right over it in the darkness, but his focus on not staring at the car made him hyper-focused on the darkness in front of him.

Willie looked around at the scene and knew that he had to go for help. He picked up the ten-dollar bill and stuck it in his pocket before heading toward the home of Charlie Fletcher, the man for whom he worked. Charlie listened to Willie intently as he turned the bill over and over in his hand. "Are you serious, Willie?" he asked. "Yes, sir," Willie answered. The look in his eyes told Charlie all he needed to hear. He told him to wait for him there on the porch and went inside to call the sheriff. When he came out, they walked together back to the scene to wait for the law to come.

They met Sheriff Belvin there, and the "Cat" set about his investigation with his deputies. Belvin could see as soon as he pulled up to the scene that the Buick that was pulled off the road was owned by Logan Dewey Forsyth, a local bootlegger. He could see the man he had been waiting to trip up and get caught lying face down in a pool of blood in the icy ditch. Charlie Fletcher stood by the road with another man he did not know; he soon found out that it was Willie Green, who had found the body. Sheriff Belvin began to question Willie and noticed that he had dried blood on his boots. Initially on the scene, Belvin felt that Willie may be a suspect. After a few moments of intense questioning, it was confirmed by Mr. Fletcher that Willie had been slaughtering hogs the past few days for him, so he was cleared.

Logan Forsyth had masqueraded as a pulpwood dealer in Durham since the war had begun in 1941 so that he could get additional gas and tire ration coupons to make his liquor runs. His front fooled few people, especially local law enforcement, whose agents were always after him. He had died from blunt-force trauma to the head and had bled out in the ditch beside his Buick. The trunk of the car was open, and there was blood spattered on the quarter panel nearest to the body, the tire and the window glass. There was a ripped $10 bill in his left front pocket of his shirt and an additional $1,100 in the right pocket of his shirt. There was $102 in the pocket of his overalls, and the victim wore a new pair of boots. It was plain to the sheriff that Logan Forsyth had been robbed and beaten to death, but it had not been cash the assailants had been after. The open trunk led them to believe that whoever had robbed and killed him had been more interested in the liquor in his trunk than the money in his pockets.

While they were working the scene, deputies went to Forsyth's house on Holloway Street to inform his wife of the murder and gather any information that she had to help with the investigation. They were familiar with the house and with Logan's wife. It had just been a few short weeks before, at the beginning of December, when they had responded to a call of domestic violence and sworn out a warrant for Logan Forsyth for smacking his wife around. She told them that Logan had left the night before, December 22, at around 7:00 p.m. saying that he had business with Osborn Roberts. Roberts was one of his "business partners," she said. Logan had said that he would be back in about thirty minutes, but that was the last time she had seen him.

Around 8:30 p.m., she said that Osborn had come to her house asking for Logan, but she told him Logan had left already and was supposed to be going to his house. Osborn waited there at the Forsyth house until 10:00 p.m. and then went home, saying that he would come back in the morning. Mrs. Forsyth told the deputies that when morning came and she had not heard from Logan, she had sent their son Junior out looking for him. Osborn Roberts came back in the morning to her house and had just left before the deputies had arrived. Roberts had told her that he thought maybe Logan had trouble with some of the people they were dealing with. Of course, when the deputies questioned Osborn Roberts, he told them nothing about their "business dealings." As far as he would tell them, they dealt in pulpwood, and he was not sure who Logan had been meeting. He had worked for Forsyth for five years as a driver and told them that he had gone to Logan's house the night before to inquire about gas for pulpwood deliveries that were scheduled.

The investigation stalled there, as no one seemed to know or want to tell the sheriff or his deputies any information. Mrs. Forsyth swore that she did not know anything about his bootlegging business. She said that they only had friends and could think of no enemies. Junior, his son, was young but had been at his dad's side since he was old enough to read because Logan could not. She did tell them that when he left the house that night, he had $2,760 on him, but that was not odd because he often carried large sums of cash. Junior would have had intimate knowledge of all of his father's business endeavors, but he told them nothing.

Osborn Roberts was jailed for several weeks as a suspect but never divulged any information. From what information Sheriff Belvin had, he deduced that Forsyth had hidden three cases of liquor under Boyce Bridge and was meeting a group of men from Hayti with the booze. Belvin told the newspapers, "Somebody set a trap to hijack his liquor, rob him of his money, and then give him the works." The beating had gone too far, and Logan Forsyth bled out in that icy ditch. Roberts was released after a few weeks for lack of any evidence, and the case remains unsolved. Most likely, whoever knows what truly happened that night is gone themselves, and the murder will remain unsolved forever.

MURDER AT DOC KING'S STORE

Two Durham police officers, Sergeant Warren and C.P. Fogleman, who were patrolling the North Durham section in the early morning hours of April 18, 1944, pulled slowly in front of King's Service Station on Roxboro Road. Everyone knew William "Doc" King in the area. He was known as a really good guy who always had a smile for everyone and was always willing to help anybody out who needed a hand. He had been dealing with burglars in the last few months and had taken on occasion to staying overnight in the store to try to scare off any would-be prowlers. The patrolmen knew this and had been stepping up patrols around his store to try to help him out. This morning, though, in the predawn hours, they shined a flashlight on the front door and immediately knew that they had a problem.

The door was slightly opened, and they could see glass broken around the doorknob. They got out of their car and walked closer to investigate. They could see glass shattered on the ground around the door. The men pulled their revolvers, and one slowly pushed the door open while the other covered him. They entered the store, scanning the scene as they went, the flashlight beam sweeping across the aisles of groceries and goods that Doc King sold there. They could see gas ration coupons scattered on the floor and the cash register open on the counter. They proceeded into the small store. As they came around the meat counter, they found a body lying in a pool of blood.

"Damn, it's Doc," Officer Fogleman said.

Doc King lay on his back with an unfired sixteen-gauge shotgun across his legs. Six bullets had torn through his body. Two had entered his body

Front view of King's Service Station after the body of William "Doc" King was discovered. *From the* Durham Sun.

under the right armpit, one through the left side of his chest, one in his stomach and another in his left lower side. Even on the scene for two officers untrained as homicide detectives, they could tell that the last bullet had been through Doc's head while he lay dying on the ground. The bullet had even scratched the concrete as it went straight through his head and skated across the floor. He wore a tan shirt with brown pants and brown socks. Several drink crates had been turned over as he fell to the ground.

The officers radioed headquarters, and soon investigators fell upon the little store. Bloodhounds were called in and soon found a scent. They set out through the woods, pulling their handlers behind them toward Cheek Road, where they found two sets of tracks. The trail led them through the low grounds to a hog pen, where they seemed to circle as if the assailants were trying to decide their next move. The tracks then moved toward Ellerbee Creek, where they parted. One set moved down the east side of a large sewer drain, while the other set moved down the other side. Eventually, they came back together and walked on top of the drain. Then they seemed to move to a fenced federal agency business about a half mile east of King's Service Station. This is where the trail ended. The government employees would not allow the dogs on the premises, and the trail could not be picked up around the fence. Whatever chance they had of tracking the killers with the dogs vanished.

Back at the service station, the police continued to investigate. King had been sleeping in a bunk that was in a loft in the back room of the store. The robbers appeared to have broken the glass and reached in to turn the latch.

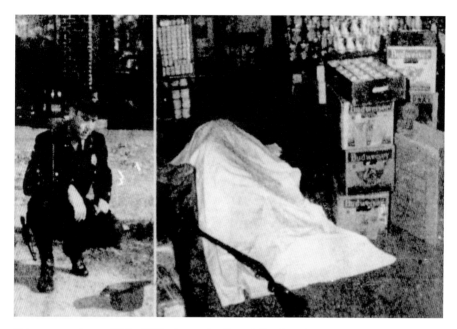

Crime scene photo of "Doc" King's murder. *From the* Durham Sun.

It was thought that when King heard the glass break, he startled the robbers as he descended the small ladder with his shotgun. The police thought that they had come for the gas rations and dropped them when they started firing. The killers then fled the scene in haste, leaving little evidence other than a gray, size 7¾ Oxford hat on the ground in the front of the store. King's body was still warm when they were investigating, leading the police to think that the murder had recently happened, but a neighbor told them he heard gunshots at around 1:30 a.m.

Doc King's wife told the police that he had no known enemies but had been robbed several times at the store. He had been surprised once while sleeping there and was badly beaten by a burglar. Years earlier, at another store he owned, he shot a burglar while he was robbing the store. She said that he had only slept in the store maybe three times since the last incident. On the night of the eighteenth, he was at Robert Massey's house playing music with a few friends and left about 9:00 p.m. Another man who lived near the service station told the investigators that around 1:30 a.m., he heard two gunshots and peered out of his window. He said he saw two men leisurely walking down Roxboro Road past his house.

Hair was taken from the hat and sent off to be analyzed, as was the .32-caliber bullets taken from King's body. The days of DNA and advanced

Left: Durham police officer pointing out the broken glass in the front door of the service station. *From the* Durham Sun.

Below: Illustration of the murder of the beloved "Doc" King. *From the* Durham Sun.

ballistic analysis were far in the future, so there was not much that could be gleaned from the evidence that was left behind. One piece of intriguing evidence was the shotgun that lay across Doc King's lifeless body. Upon inspection, they found that it was empty, and there were no shells for the gun anywhere in the store. King's wife told the police that it was possible that someone had borrowed the gun for hunting and had returned it empty. King may have thought that it was loaded as he confronted the robbers. Another theory is that the gunmen killed King and saw the shotgun propped in the corner and planted it on him. They may have been planning to use self-defense as a reason for the slaying if they were caught.

Another factor that bothered the police investigators was that in almost all cases when a burglary turned into a shootout, the suspects would fire their weapons moving backward, shooting while trying to flee. In the case of the King murder, the wounds indicated that the shots were fired while the shooter moved toward King, ending in the kill shot standing directly over him. It appeared that the killers "bore him malice," as police officials stated later. Police Chief H.E. King felt at the time that the murder would be difficult to solve. Durham's population had grown during the war, and there were many transients passing through. Military deserters who were running from authorities were resorting to crime all over the country in an attempt to get home, so there had been a spike in crime nationwide.

"Those were not normal times," Chief King said later. "We had a greatly increased population in Durham then, and not enough officers to enforce the law. New faces were appearing daily, with so much fluctuation."

The chief was right about the difficulty of solving the crime. It never got past the initial investigation, although the Durham Police Department kept the case open for many years and tried to follow all of the leads. Without many of the modern investigation tools that we have today, there was so little evidence that the case went cold and was finally closed. Doc King made his mark on the neighborhood, though, and was remembered for generations as a kind and generous man. His killers slipped off into the darkness and were never found.

CASUALTY OF ANOTHER WAR

Booker T. Spicely waited at the bus stop at Pettigrew and Fayetteville Streets, making small talk with a woman and her small child. A six-foot-tall Black man from Philadelphia in a crisp army uniform, he stood out in Durham at the height of the Second World War. Although born in Blackstone, Virginia, the thirty-four-year-old Private Spicely felt somewhat out of place in the South. Back home in Philadelphia, where he had grown up, things were different. He didn't feel like a second-class citizen, especially in his uniform, which he wore with pride.

When the bus stopped, Booker stepped aside and let the woman and her child board first. Then he followed them to the back of the bus, where there were some empty seats available. Booker took a seat on the second-to-last row as the bus drove toward its next stop. When the doors opened again, a group of soldiers stepped on the bus and looked down the aisle.

"Hey! Move to the back row!" the bus driver barked at Booker. The comment struck him like he had been slapped, and his immediate reaction was to respond.

"I thought I was fighting this war for democracy. We're both wearing the same uniform," Booker replied. "I don't see why I have to move back. In Pennsylvania, we pay one time and sit where we please."

"Shut up or get off the bus," was the driver's response.

Being in Durham, North Carolina, he was a long way from home and was not used to the treatment he had received since he had been down south. Although racism existed in Philadelphia, he was freer to move about the city and not be treated with such disdain and disrespect everywhere he went. It had been grating on him, and he had reached his limit with the surly bus driver. He looked around him at the other passengers, who were either trying to ignore the situation or looked at him with a kind of pity. Even the white soldiers who had gotten on the bus seemed to agree with him. He turned and looked at the young mother, though, and her eyes begged him to just move back and defuse the situation.

Booker reluctantly moved back, but as he sat, he continued to trade barbs with the driver. "I thought I was fighting a war for democracy, but it looks like it doesn't work like that down here," he said. "Lousy 4-Fer," Booker mumbled under his breath, expressing disgust at the physical fitness of the driver who was obviously ineligible for military service yet was ordering him around.

"I don't care what you say or like," the bus driver said. "If you don't like it, then come and get me." Booker could see his eyes flaming with rage in the large mirror above the steering wheel.

"You come back here!" Booker yelled back.

"Come up here. I've got something that will cool you off," he snarled back, getting more and more excited. Private Spicely began to think better of his verbal parrying with the driver. Everyone on the bus looked uncomfortable, and he knew, although he thought he was right, he was in a position that was not going to be the one that came out on top no matter what happened. He could see the cards stacked against him, and as the bus neared the bus stop on Club Boulevard and Fourth Street, now Berkley Street, at Walltown, he decided he better take his leave and wait for another bus to come by. As the bus stopped, Private Booker Spicely stood up and took his hat off of his head.

"If I done you any harm bus driver, I beg your pardon. I didn't mean any harm with what I said." With that, he stepped out of the back door of the bus, replaced his hat and looked around. He thought that he had avoided any further confrontation, but his apology had seemed to only make the driver angrier. As Booker was stepping off the bottom step and putting his hat back on, the driver, to the horror of the other riders, produced a revolver and leaped from his seat and down the front steps. When he hit the ground, he aimed and shot Booker in the chest just as he was turning to see what was going on. The bullet ripped through his body, and Booker turned to run away from his assailant. The driver leveled his aim and fired into the fleeing man's back. Booker fell, mortally wounded, and rolled into a ditch as he struggled for life.

Club Boulevard, where the body of Booker T. Spicely lay dying before being rushed a few blocks away to Watts Hospital. *Author's collection.*

Hearing gunshots, several people who lived on Club Boulevard called the police, and they came quickly to the scene of the crime. They found the bus driver, Herman Lee Council, waiting for them. He described what happened, and to everyone's surprise, the police allowed him to get back on the bus and finish his route before turning himself in later. Booker was in really bad shape and needed help badly. Just a few blocks from where he had been shot was Watts Hospital. But when he was taken there, they refused to help him. Watts was a whites-only hospital, and rules were rules they said. They did take the time to get a quick blood sample from him so a toxicology report could be done to see if he was intoxicated at the time of the altercation. After the blood sample, he was taken to Duke Hospital, but by the time he arrived it was too late. When the officers got him to Duke Hospital, Booker was barely clinging to life. The hospital staff went to work trying in vain to save him. Soon after arriving, he expired. Somewhere just a few blocks away, the Duke Power bus, driven by his killer, was picking up and dropping off riders as if nothing had happened.

As he promised, Herman Lee Council turned himself in but was promptly bailed out by his employer, the Duke Power Company. He was tried two weeks later for second-degree murder. The state, represented by solicitor

Booker T. Spicely was shot just a few blocks from Watts Hospital, but they refused to treat him because he was Black. *Durham County Library, North Carolina Collection.*

R.H. Sykes, was asking for the maximum of thirty years in prison. The first witness was city employee A.C. DeBruyne, who mapped out the route of the bus and explained to the jury where the bus was located at the time of the incident. The next witness was a corporal from Camp Butner who had been on the bus and testified that there were words exchanged between the two men and that Spicely had exited the bus and was shot on the sidewalk.

Dr. George Culbreth of Duke Hospital gave a detailed testimony of Spicely's condition upon arrival at the hospital. "His shirt was bloody and partly torn off. There were two jagged wounds in the body, one on the left side and one near the stomach. One bullet went through the man's Army dog tag. One of the bullets went all the way through the body while the other lodged in his back." Dr. Culberth described how he took the bullet from his back and noted powder marks around the wound. He testified that there were no weapons found on Booker Spicely.

Over and over, witness after witness, testified that although words were exchanged, Booker was complying with the driver's instructions and had exited the bus to avoid any further conflict. When Council took the stand, he testified that Spicely had put his hand in his pocket and made a move toward him when he had gotten off the bus, but there were no witnesses who corroborated that testimony. The all-white jury spent only twenty-eight minutes deciding if he was guilty or not. They decided the latter, and Council was a free man. He went back to driving his bus as if nothing happened along the same route.

The tragedy was indicative of the problem the nation would continue to struggle with for many years. Booker T. Spicely left his home and was

In death, Spicely had a significant impact on the growth of the NAACP in North Carolina and helped shed light on the oppressive nature of Jim Crow laws North Carolina and the South. *Author's collection.*

proudly serving his country in the nation's darkest hour, yet there were large parts of the country where he was treated as less than a second-class citizen. Just as Booker bristled at the thought of taking a back seat, his death, along with many others, would soon give many people pause as they talked about the question of civil rights in America. Many people who had never dealt with the situation would find themselves firmly on the side of either freedom or oppression.

AXE MURDER OF ROSA CROCKETT

November 7, 1945, was a nice sunny day in Durham. Forty-two-year-old Rosa Crockett sat on her front porch at 404 Poplar Avenue on the east side of Durham. She rocked back and forth and watched the children of the neighborhood play down the street. Rosa was poor, like everyone else in the little neighborhood, but she was happy. She supplemented her income like many people by selling illegal whiskey, which came down from the Hayti area of Durham. She had just sold some the day before, and knowing that she had some cash in the cigar box in her wardrobe made her feel just a little better. It was a good day. She closed her eyes and leaned her head back to take a deep breath and enjoy the moment. Then everything went black.

Rosa's neighbor was standing in front of her kitchen sink washing dishes when she heard a commotion from across the street. She leaned forward and craned her neck out to see a small group of people gathered around Rosa's front porch. She could see her sitting in her rocking chair, but the way she was sitting seemed off. Men stood around her and looked her over. She sat slumped in the rocking chair with the back of her head badly beaten in, and a small axe was lying in the grass off the side of the porch. Soon, detectives from the Durham Police Department were on scene.

Frank McCrea and his partner, Clyde Cox, began questioning the neighbors and searching the house. Their investigation led them to Wee Wee Grill on Pettigrew Street, where they talked to one of the regular patrons, Delores Tatum. She told the detectives that the night before the murder, they had been at Rosa's house. Delores told them that she had been at the

Wee Wee Grill when a young man named Aaron Huggins had come in and started talking to her and her friend Alease Smith. Huggins told them there was a place they could get some bootleg whiskey and could have a drink without anyone bothering them. They agreed to follow him, and the three ended up at the home of Rosa Crockett. Delores told them that they had been drinking there for several hours when her and Alease left Aaron there and went home. Huggins was their main suspect, but he had disappeared. The detectives had few of the resources that officers have today to track him, but they promised themselves to not let the death of Rosa Crockett go without justice.

Years went by, and the detectives gathered more information that seemed to point to Aaron Huggins. They wanted the chance to question him, but he was a ghost. Every lead seemed to come to a dead end. Almost ten years after the murder, they got one final tip. They heard that Aaron Huggins was back in Durham. Sources told them that he was at a woman's house on Alston Avenue, so McCrea and Cox made their move. They arrived at the house and could hear the sound of splitting wood in the backyard. Ironically, as they came around the house, they found Huggins, axe in hand, chopping wood for his girlfriend, who had just moved to Durham.

He looked up at them, and they identified themselves. They told Huggins that they wanted to speak to him about the death of Rosa Crockett, and he said he knew it already. He admitted to the murder almost immediately and told them that he wanted to get it off of his chest. He described to them that he had been arrested several times since the murder, and each time he thought for sure he was going to be linked to the murder. But it never happened, so he thought he was fine. They took him to the house where the murder had taken place, and he walked them through the crime.

He said he had seen where Rosa kept the money from the sale of the whiskey. She had put it in a cigar box in a wardrobe in her bedroom. He was planning on knocking her out and stealing the money. He came up from the back of the house and saw a small hatchet by the backdoor outside the kitchen. He snuck around the house and saw her sitting in the rocking chair. When he struck her, he said he thought it would just knock her out, but he knew immediately that he had taken her life. He proceeded into the house and took about fifty dollars from the cigar box. He showed the officers where the wardrobe had once stood. McCrea and Cox placed him under arrest and took him downtown to be booked and tried for murder. They had kept working the cold case, and it paid off, along with the revelation that he had served time in South Carolina for killing a man.

Detectives Frank McCrea and Clyde Cox did not give up on the case and finally brought Aaron Huggins to justice. *From the* Durham Sun.

Huggins, after speaking to an attorney, changed his story. He pleaded not guilty. He said that he had only given a confession so that he could just serve a few months, and the police would leave him alone. He had not provided a written statement because he could not read or write. On the stand, he did not do himself any favors. He admitted that the detectives did not coerce him in any way and that they had been nice to him throughout the process. Asked by the prosecutor why he had confessed before, he said, "At the time I wasn't thinking when I told them. I didn't think then that I would get much time or would be tried for a capital crime." The statement was damning, and his attorney soon counseled him to change his plea to guilty, which would ensure that he would receive a life sentence.

The judge at sentencing told his attorney, "Your client has been advised well, and this was, in my opinion, the safest course to be pursued by him." To detectives McCrea and Cox, he said, "The community ought to feel that the

Durham Police Department has rendered a valuable service in this case, and the two officers testifying should be commended for their fairness, efficiency, and accuracy. I think the public should know this."

The two men, trailblazers for later African American law enforcement officers, did not give up. They would not give up on the cold case and made sure that justice was served for Rosa Crockett, who died while she rocked on her porch. Huggins died in jail years later but avoided the electric chair.

SHOOTOUT IN PATTERSON TOWNSHIP

On the cold morning of December 22, 1949, Deputies Jack Walters and J.M. Mangum responded to a call in Patterson Township, an African American community just south of Durham. They had been told that fifty-year-old Oscar Surrette had been "acting queer" for the last few days and that he had been pacing around his farmhouse with his double-barreled shotgun yelling at anyone passing by. Reports said that he had even shot at some of his neighbors, but they could not confirm that information as they pulled up to the house.

The two deputies surveyed the house from their car and saw no movement. The wind blew outside, and they watched the branches of the trees and bushes sway around them. It was a peaceful scene, but they knew there could still be danger. When they exited the car, they went first to the front door and knocked, with no response. They milled around on the porch for a moment looking into the windows and seeing no movement. They decided to walk around the back of the house and knock on the back door and see if they could see anything from the back windows. The house was set on a slope, with the front level to the ground and the back elevated on blocks. The deputies walked up the back steps and knocked, but again there was no answer. They looked up at the windows and decided that they could not see anything from their position there. The men agreed to go next door and start asking questions to the neighbors to get more information on what was going on when they were suddenly taken by surprise by a crazed Oscar Surrette.

LINCOLN HOSPITAL, DURHAM, N. C.

Deputy J.M. Mangum probably saved Deputy Jack Walters's life by rushing him to Lincoln Hospital after being shot by Oscar Surrette. *Durham County Library, North Carolina Collection.*

Jack Walters saw him first stooped over, standing in the darkness under the house. When they made eye contact, Surrette moved toward Walters, raising his shotgun as he moved. Walters reached for his revolver, and Surrette fired a shot, hitting him in the right forearm and his holster and belt. Walters fell back screaming in pain as Surrette took a shot at Mangum and missed. He retreated into his house while reloading. Mangum, thinking quickly, instead of engaging in a gun battle, grabbed Walters under the arms and pulled him back to the cover of their car. Walters held his right arm close to his body with his left hand as he winced and moaned in pain. More shots rang out from the house as Mangum pulled Walter in the back of the car and drove him to Lincoln Hospital in hopes of saving him from bleeding to death.

From the hospital, Mangum called in the situation to Sheriff Cat Belvin, who immediately went into action, forming a posse. He grabbed a few available deputies, a couple of Durham police officers and a highway patrolman on the way. When they arrived at the house, they saw the same serene farmhouse that Walters and Mangum had rolled up to earlier, but the scene did not last. As they exited their cars, shots began to ring out from the farmhouse. The lawmen began to scatter and take up firing positions behind trees and squad cars while returning fire.

Oscar Surrette laid down withering and accurate fire with his double-barreled shotgun but had to stop frequently to reload. He moved from window to window, unleashing a deadly barrage. The lawmen began to get a sense of timing between the shots and moved closer to the house, dodging from covered position to covered position along the way. Durham officer Frank McRea crept toward the back of the house along with patrolman R.H. McNeil. Suddenly, the back door flew open, and Surrette bolted out, knelt and fired at McRea. He was able to avoid taking the blast directly by turning to the side. The pellets ripped through his legs, thigh and hip. Surrette turned and fired at McNeil, who ducked and had the hat shot off his head. Surrette turned to run back into the cabin and took a bullet in the hip. He limped back inside as a hail of bullets struck around him and slammed the door.

The officers had positioned themselves close enough to the house to deploy tear gas grenades through the windows. They communicated with one another around the house, and the next time Surrette stopped shooting to reload, several of the lawmen flung themselves against the side of the house and tossed the grenades through the windows. They could hear the smoke grenades' distinct popping sound, and they moved back to the safety of their previous positions. In moments, they could hear Oscar Surrette choking and coughing from inside the house. The wind whipped against the house through the shattered windows, soon pushing the gas out into the yard and forcing the lawmen to retreat from their positions to a farther distance from the house. Sheriff Belvin was concerned that the gas would dissipate before it forced Surrette out of his house. His fears were soon dissuaded when Oscar Surrette appeared again, coming out of the back door choking and pawing at his eyes.

"Don't kill him, boys!" the sheriff yelled as they moved in on him and put him in custody.

"People have been after me. They have been trying to kill me!" he cried over and over again as they dragged him, handcuffed and bleeding from the hip, to one of the patrol cars in his yard.

Before the gunfight ended that day, three officers and one neighbor had been wounded. All of them survived their injuries. Oscar Surrette was wounded in the hip and was in critical condition for several days in the hospital. It was a miracle after so many shots had been fired that no one was killed. Surrette claimed again in court that everyone was after him—the police, his family and his neighbors were all in it together against him. He accused his neighbor of firing at him with an "aircraft gun." In a modern courtroom, the issue of his mental fitness would have surely been brought up by his attorney and would have been taken into account, but in early 1950, he was sentenced to sixteen years in prison for the shootings. He would serve less than that. Oscar Surrette was paroled in 1956 and, by all accounts, led a law-abiding life after his release. The wild shootout south of the city had been the stuff that legends were made of. Several of the officers involved would go on to have illustrious careers in Durham and put their stamp on the history of the city.

JUST A RIDE

When Lawrence Jackson got the call from Marie Penny asking for a ride to work at the First Presbyterian Church on East Main Street, he didn't think much of it. He had known Marie for many years. Years before, she had met and married her husband, John W. Penny. They had been friends throughout, and Lawrence knew that sometimes Marie just needed a break from John, who had been known to be cantankerous and mean at times. That day on July 21, 1954, would turn out to be anything but a normal day or just another ride to work for a friend.

Jackson picked Marie up at her house and began driving toward the church in his Chevrolet when he noticed John Penny coming up fast behind them in his Buick. He could tell by the look on his face that he was incredibly angry. Lawrence asked Marie why he was so mad, and she said she did not know. He had probably gotten it into his head that they must be up to something, but she said that he should know by now because they have been friends for so long. Lawrence Jackson drove on, trying to ignore him as he snarled in his rear-view mirror. Marie turned around in her seat and looked at her husband, seeing the rage on his face.

Jackson was anticipating a confrontation when they got to the church but hoped that when he saw where they were going, he would calm down. They never made it that far. As he pulled through the intersection of Elm Street and Fayetteville Street, Penny made his move. He swung his Buick around Jackson's Chevy and slammed into the driver's side, forcing the car onto the curb. Jackson could hardly believe what had happened as he put the car in park, angry that his car had been damaged and preparing himself to confront Penny about hitting his car. Before he could open his door, John Penny was coming around his car with a knife in his hand. Marie screamed from the passenger side of the car, and Lawrence slapped the door lock button and reached for the hand crank to roll the window up. It was too late, and Penny was at his window before he could get it halfway up. He reached in and began slashing with the knife. Jackson slid as far as he could away from Penny, smushing Marie against the passenger side door trying to avoid the flashing blade.

Jackson reached under his car seat as Penny slashed and struck at him with his knife and groped for the door lock with his free hand. Lawrence Jackson's fingers finally found their target, pulled a .38-caliber German Luger from under the seat and began to fire at his attacker.

The first bullet struck Penny's right, which wielded the knife. It knocked the knife out of his hand, which dropped onto the seat of the car. The second bullet struck his left arm, and the third bullet struck John Penny under his left eye and exited the back of his head. Penny slumped to the ground by the car, dead. The fevered attack was over, and Lawrence and Marie huddled on the passenger side of the car looking across the front seat at broken glass, splattered blood and the knife lying in a small pool of blood on the front seat where moments before Jackson had sat driving his friend to work.

When the police arrived, it seemed like it would be an open-and-shut case of self-defense. "What was he supposed to do, just let Penny murder him as he sat helplessly in the car?" As the squad car pulled up, Jackson approached their car and said, "I'm the one you are looking for, I did it." The officers surveyed the scene and could see the damage to the cars and the positions of the vehicles. They could see the half-open window and the blood and the knife on the seat. They could see that the story Jackson told them was accurate and that the events he had described had gone down just as he had said. Marie Penny corroborated his story, but there was just one problem for the officers. Soon, Lawrence Jackson found himself in handcuffs in the back of the police car, charged with second-degree murder.

Once again, the "unwritten law" came into play. The way the police and the district attorney saw it, if Jackson was having an inappropriate relationship with Marie Penny, then John Penny was justified in attacking him. As they investigated, they had more questions about the relationship and the situation that led up to the killing. It was discovered that Jackson's wife was out of town at the time. Did she know about these "rides"? Why did he have the gun under the seat? Was he expecting trouble?

Opposite: Crime scene photos from the death of John Penny. *From the* Durham Sun.

Above: Lawrence Jackson's car after the altercation that led to Penny's death. *From the* Durham Sun.

When he went to trial, witness after witness came forward in a full-throated defense of both Lawrence and Marie. Even the pastor of the church where she worked testified that they had been friends for a long time and that both were beyond reproach. Jackson's wife knew of the friendship, and she trusted her husband. Lawrence testified at the trial that he was not looking for any trouble the day of the incident. He took the gun from the house because his wife was not home, and he was afraid the house would be burglarized and he would lose it. The jury contemplated the situation and found him not guilty of second-degree murder. Had they believed that the "unwritten law" had been violated, as in the Wiles case, they may have sent Lawrence Jackson to jail for the murder of John Penny. The many character witnesses saved him from jail and her from a besmirched reputation.

MURDER-SUICIDE ON ELDER STREET

Dr. Robert Coker had a bad feeling as he pulled up in front of the nondescript brick apartment building at 2215 Elder Street on March 29, 1960. Robert was the son of the renowned head of the Zoology Department at the University of North Carolina, Dr. R.E. Coker, and the brother of Dr. Coit Coker, a botanist in his own right. Robert was also a faculty member at the School of Public Health at the University of North Carolina. He was at the apartment on Elder Street because he had become increasingly worried about his brother Coit in the last few days and felt like he needed to check on him.

Coit Coker had been on the same track as his father and elder brother to take his place in academia before the Japanese bombed Pearl Harbor in December 1941. He then stepped back from his education and became an officer in the U.S. Navy. For the first few years of the war, he trained for what would be the greatest invasion in the history of the world. On June 6, 1944, he landed as a naval gunfire liaison officer with the 116th Infantry on Omaha Beach. That day, he earned a Purple Heart for shrapnel wounds and a Silver Star for gallantry in the face of the enemy. After the war, he returned home to his education and earned his doctorate in botany. He taught classes at the University of Puerto Rico, where he met his wife, Ann Carrasquillo. On the surface, he looked like he was doing great, but his brother knew better. He had never been the same since his experience on the beaches of France, and his brother noticed the small but increasing changes early on.

By the spring of 1960, as Robert stood at the door of his apartment one morning, it had become clearer to everyone else. He lost his job in 1956 in Puerto Rico and had moved back to Durham. For the past four years, he had been unemployed, while his wife worked as a nurse at Duke Hospital. Coit had increasingly become paranoid and jealous of Ann and was easily agitated at times. When Robert called his brother on Monday night and then again on Tuesday morning, he became concerned that something had happened to him. After knocking several times with no answer, he took a deep breath and slowly pushed open the door.

What he saw immediately concerned him. In the corner of the hall was a shotgun propped in the corner, and he could see blood splattered on the floor. He turned on the light switch and stepped inside, calling his brother's name. At the end of the hall was the door to the bedroom, which stood open, but the room was dark; he could not make out anything from where he stood. He called out for Ann as he moved down the hall. He looked into the small bathroom off the hall as he passed and could see a bloody footprint on the floor by the shower. A heavy weight dropped in his stomach. It was not fear. It was the anticipation of what he would find in the dark at the end of the hall.

Robert pushed open the door and turned the switch on in the bedroom, exposing a ghastly sight. Ann lay on the floor face down in a pool of blood. She wore a pink slip, and her bedroom slippers lay by her feet. Coit lay on his back across the bed with a clean cut across his throat and a pool of blood soaked into the bed under him. Robert covered his mouth and stepped back out of the room. He immediately called the police and waited outside for them to arrive. Soon the apartment was abuzz with detectives and police officers investigating the deaths.

They found that Ann had been killed at least two days before by a shotgun blast to the chest. There was a spent shotgun shell on the floor in the bedroom, and the shotgun had a shell in the chamber that had been snapped but had not fired. After speaking with neighbors, the police discovered that around 4:00 a.m., they were awoken by a strange noise. Then they distinctly heard a woman say, "You hurt me! You hurt me!" Then there was nothing. Attributing it to either neighborhood noises or just a marital squabble, they went back to bed and thought nothing of it. They had not seen the Cokers since then, but they said that it was not uncommon.

The police immediately thought it looked like a murder-suicide. It was obvious to the crime scene investigators that Coit had died at least two days after Ann. The theory was that he had shot her and tried to shoot himself

Left: Durham police investigate the deaths of Dr. Coker and his wife, Ann. *From the* Durham Sun.

Below: Robert Coker examines his brother Coit's wallet while helping Durham police with the investigation. *From the* Durham Sun.

Opposite: The apartment where Dr. Coker killed his wife and then himself is now used by Duke Healthcare. *Author's collection.*

but that there had been a misfire, and he propped the shotgun in the corner and spent the next two days in the apartment with his wife's body on the floor in the bedroom. At some point in the hours before Robert had shown up to look for him, he had gone into the bedroom, sat on the bed and cut his own throat. There was only one problem with the scenario that the police put forward: they could not find the blade that he had used to cut his throat anywhere in the apartment.

The mystery was temporary. Two days later, the medical examiner found a straight razor in the dead man's pocket as he prepared him for interment. Dr. Coit Coker had apparently sat on the bed and cut his throat from ear to ear and then calmly placed the blade into his trouser pocket. This was just one last final piece of evidence of the demons that Coit must have been experiencing internally. From all accounts, he descended into madness following the trauma of the war. In a time when it was seen as unmanly or weak to seek help, Dr. Coker slipped through the cracks and took his wife with him in a tragic conclusion to their lives.

MURDER OF DEPUTY THOMAS LAND

The Nelson community in Durham County has long faded into obscurity, but in October 1972, the now bustling area around where Miami Boulevard and Highway 54 meet was once a tiny crossroads in the middle of tobacco fields. In one of the most rural parts of the county at the time, there was still opportunity for businesses that could see the future. There was money in the area even then. Close to Raleigh and surrounded by farmers who needed a place to deposit their money from their crops, Wachovia Bank saw the need to build a bank in the area. Until they could get a permanent structure, they had a trailer set up to take deposits from the farmers and workers and cash checks. A small white trailer with a covered porch served as the center of commerce for the little community.

On the fifth of October, what seemed to be a routine day for the tellers and the manager of Wachovia was turned upside down in an instant. Shortly before 1:00 p.m., the door burst open, and a masked gunman carrying an M1 .30-caliber carbine rifle came toward the tellers.

"Everyone put your hands up!" he shouted as he threw a burlap sack to one of the tellers, ordering her to fill it with money. Holt Anderson, the branch manager, came out to see what the commotion was and found himself looking down the barrel of the rifle. As the gunman turned momentarily to make sure Anderson had his hands up, one of the tellers hit the silent bank alarm and proceeded to fill the bag. When she was done, the robber herded them into the bathroom and locked them in. There was a sigh of relief in the cramped bathroom. Although locked in the small space, their experience was over, they thought. Moments later, they were jarred back to reality when they heard five to six gunshots from inside the bank. The bathroom door was abruptly opened again, and Anderson was grabbed and pulled out, leaving the tellers frightened and confused.

There was no way they could have known what had transpired in the few moments that passed since the teller hit the alarm. As soon as it went through, the call was sent out to the nearest sheriff's deputies in the area. Less than a mile away, Deputy Jerry Wilkerson, along with his partner, twenty-five-year-old rookie Thomas Land, who were patrolling Olde Raleigh Road, responded to the call. As they pulled up to the bank, Wilkerson looked over, and Land and told him to be careful. Deputy Wilkerson called back to dispatch that they were on location, and they got out of the car and headed toward the door. Wilkerson once more warned Land to be cautious as they stepped onto the porch. As Wilkerson, who was in the lead, opened the door, he came face to face with the gunman, unmasked and holding a military-style rifle pointing it in his direction.

"Drop it! Drop it!" the robber shouted at Wilkerson. Wilkerson slammed the door shut and yelled for Thomas to take cover as he darted to the patrol car. He could hear several shots ring out behind him as he slid in the gravel and crawled to the back of the car. He moved toward the back of the car and, with pistol drawn, stuck his head up to assess the situation. He could see the shattered glass of the bank door but could not see his partner. Wilkerson moved back to the front of the car and accessed the radio to call for assistance. He called out for Deputy Land, but there was no answer. Wilkerson rose and fired one shot at the bank door and was met by a return shot that shattered the back windshield of the patrol car. Glass flew through the air and cut his face up, dropping him back down into cover.

Meanwhile, in the bank, the gunman had gone back to the bathroom where he had locked his hostages and grabbed Anderson out. He dragged him to the door and, pointing the rifle at the stunned officer behind the car, demanded that he throw out his revolver and give himself up. A tense, silent moment followed, but Wilkerson stood up and tossed his gun on the ground. The robber asked him if he had called for help, and Wilkerson said no, hoping that the lie could buy him some time. He was next ordered to handcuff himself to the rail of the bank's porch. Wilkerson walked to the porch with his hands up, never taking his eyes off his captor, and handcuffed himself to the rail.

"Toss the key away!" the robber yelled as he held his rifle on Wilkerson. He complied and tossed the key into the gravel. The gunman dragged Anderson to the bank-owned blue Plymouth and instructed him to drive. Wilkerson watched as they drove away, heading north on Highway 70 toward Raleigh. The gravity of the last few moments set in as he stood bleeding handcuffed to the rail. He still was not sure of the fate of his partner, but as he looked around, he could see the feet of Deputy Land sticking out from the other side of the porch. He called to him again, but there was still no answer.

In a few moments, one of the bank tellers came out of the bank and asked if anybody was hurt. "Lady, for God's sake, get my keys lying over there and let me get uncuffed!" Deputy Wilkerson barked at her. She hurriedly came down the steps and grabbed his keys. Wilkerson fumbled with them for a moment until he freed himself and ran back to his car. He called out again on the radio, giving a description of the car and the bank robber. He also advised that there was a hostage. He then raced back over to the porch and knelt beside Thomas Land to check on him. It was apparent immediately that he was dead. Twenty-five-year-old Thomas "Tommy" Land, who had served in Vietnam as a Seabee and had only been on the force since August 16 of that same year, was gone. His murderer was on the run, and Wilkerson could only wish that he had the chance to get in on the pursuit. He would not have the chance.

Roberts Brooks had been driving past the bank when he saw the officers running toward the door. He saw Wilkerson turn to flee and saw Land jump off the side of the porch after being shot. He drove to a gas station near the bank and ran inside. He yelled for the cashier to call the Sheriff's Department, that there was a bank robbery taking place, and he was sure that someone had been shot. Brooks went back outside to his car in time to see the blue Plymouth pull off from the bank with two men inside and head north on Highway 70. At another gas station farther down the road, North Carolina state trooper Stanley Flythe heard the follow-up call on the radio and was on the lookout when the Plymouth drove by.

In the blue car, Anderson nervously followed the instructions of his captor. He nervously gripped the wheel as the gunman instructed him to drive slowly and obey the traffic laws so they would not draw attention. Anderson saw the highway patrol car sitting at the gas station they passed and saw it in the rear-view mirror pulling out and beginning to follow them. His captor noticed too and began to look back over his shoulder at the patrol car as it drew closer. Holt Anderson's heart almost leaped out of his chest when he heard the siren and saw the blue lights.

"Pull over," he was ordered by the gunman. He did, and the highway patrolman pulled up behind them. "Tell him to come here," Anderson was

Crime scene photo from the bank entrance where Deputy Land was shot. *From the* Durham Sun.

told. He looked at his captor and pistol that he was holding on him and the rifle that was beside him on the seat. "Motion him to the window with your hand," he said. Anderson complied, held his hand out of the window and motioned the trooper to come to the window. His eyes and the trooper's eyes met in the rear-view mirror, and he could see him shake his head no. Trooper Flythe had no intention of approaching the car until backup came. He knew that he would be vulnerable in the open and could wind up in a gunfight with the suspect, who had already shown his willingness to shoot. On top of that, there was a hostage who would be in the middle of the gunfight. Flythe stayed put and worked the radio, trying to get other officers to respond. Before they could reach him, the blue car once again pulled out on Highway 70 and continued toward Raleigh.

Trooper Flythe continued the pursuit, and soon he was joined by several other patrol cars. They were ready to make their move. When the car came to the intersection of Highway 50 and Highway 70 in Crabtree Valley, Anderson was instructed to head north on Highway 50. The law enforcement cars followed closely behind. Anderson grew more and more nervous and could tell that the gunman was reaching the end of his rope. As

Left: The pursuit of the bank robber and murderer ended in Wake County. *From the* Durham Sun.

Right: Bennie Lee Glenn in custody. *From the* Durham Sun.

they came to a country road, he was instructed to turn off and pull the car sideways across the road. Anderson knew that he intended to have a final gun battle with the officers and had no intention of complying.

As he pulled off the road, he took the opportunity to grab the hand that held the gun and wrestle it from the robber. The troopers behind them could see the struggle, and as the car careened into a ditch, they were out of their cars already and on top of the getaway car. They dragged the gunman out of the car and took him into custody, and he was soon on his way back to Durham County.

The perpetrator was twenty-five-year-old Bennie Lee Glenn of Durham. He was booked and charged with armed robbery, assault with a deadly weapon, kidnapping and murder. At trial, Glenn's defense attorney conceded the charges except for murder. There was some issue with the evidence, as the fatal shot was deemed to have entered Deputy Land's open mouth and exited the back of his head, killing him instantly. Testimony from Robert Brooks identified Land as jumping from the porch as he drove by. Prosecutors tried to explain that the movement he saw could have easily been misconstrued as Land *falling* from the porch instead after the fatal shot. The defense tried to accuse Wilkerson of firing his pistol wildly in the direction of the bank and killing Land in error as he tried to communicate with Wilkerson from his position by the front porch. Criminal evidence experts testified that the shots had come from a rifle and not a pistol.

At the conclusion of the trial, Glenn was convicted on all but the murder charge. One lone juror held out, and Glenn avoided life in prison. He was sentenced to 115 years in prison but was released on an appeal in 1989 after serving only seventeen years. Jerry Wilkerson left the Sheriff's Department a few years later and served many years as an investigator for the Durham Police Department. Today, a picture of Deputy Thomas Land still hangs in the Sheriff's Department as a memorial to a good man and a promising deputy whose life was cut short before he was able to make a lasting impact on his community. As is usual, tragedy tends to be an effective teacher, as the robbery has been used to teach officers about the dangers of approaching high-risk situations. It also illustrated a shift in the mentality of law enforcement in Durham County. A new day had dawned in the county, where relative safety and down-home policing had been sufficient for years compared to the high crime tactics of the city police. No longer could law enforcement take anything for granted when they approached a situation anywhere in Durham after that day.

ONE SHOT FIRED

L arry Bullock was a twenty-five-year-old Durham police investigator on April 29, 1976. He had only been on the force for three years, but he was a fire eater and a damn good cop. Lieutenant Jerry Johnson had recognized his talent and his knack for police work and had encouraged him to join the DPD Vice Squad just three months before that April day. Larry had jumped at the chance to make a real difference in his community. He had dreamed of a more challenging and exciting role with the department. Young and married, he and his wife, Brenda, lived in Bahama, which was a little north of Durham, and Larry saw the dangers of the steady flow of drugs on the streets. He wanted to make a difference.

On that April evening, following a tip they had received of drug dealing around the campus of North Carolina Central University, Bullock, Lieutenant Johnson, Sergeant J.C. Fuller and Investigator D.W. Clark got a warrant to search an apartment on Pilot Street. Dressed in plainclothes, they proceeded to the door and positioned themselves to the side and away from directly in front of the door. Bullock knocked on the door. From inside they heard a voice call out, "Who is it?"

"Durham Police Department," Johnson announced. They heard a mad scrambling inside the apartment moving away from the front room. The officers entered the apartment and could see the occupants flee into a back room. Bullock led the charge after them, and as he reached the door to the back room, one single shot rang out in the dark, crowded apartment. Larry Bullock fell on the floor, struck in the chest. The other officers took up strategic positions and called for the gunman to come out with his hands in the air. Soon, a young man came out of the room and placed the gun on the ground. He was taken into custody along with several others.

Larry was rushed to Duke Hospital and pronounced dead at 10:15 p.m., just forty-five short minutes since he had stood by the front door to serve the initial warrant. Durham Police Chief John Kindice was at the hospital when he passed and wept by his bedside. As Kindice left the hospital, he was confronted by members of the local media, and with red bloodshot eyes, he gave an emotional plea to his community. "What brings society to a point that we are losing so many officers?" He was referring to Bullock's death as well as the recent deaths of two North Carolina highway patrolmen. "These people were not big-time pushers. It's not like they were facing twenty years in prison if they got caught. What prompts this vicious type of reaction?" In his mind, he could just not see the justification for the slaying of such a good and decent man. He walked past them shaking his head. Bullock had been killed in his prime. He was well liked and had a bright future ahead of him.

The men whom the warrant was originally for were John McCombs Jr. and Edward Moore. Both men had been present in the apartment along with several young women. McCombs was the shooter. As they had fled to the back room, he had turned and shot into the apartment at the officers, and the one shot struck Bullock in the heart. Enough marijuana was found in the apartment to warrant a felony charge, but as Kindice had pointed out, it was nowhere near the charges McCombs would then face with the slaying of a police officer. There had not been an officer killed in the line of duty in Durham for forty years.

When Larry Bullock was laid to rest at a little country cemetery near Rougemont, four hundred people attended. A Durham police honor guard stood at attention while Chief Kindince spoke to those gathered. "We loved Larry very much," Chief Kindice said, voice shaking. "He had a large family," he paused, "350,000 throughout the nation—and all of them will miss him." Tears began to form in the chief's eyes as he looked out on the crowd of mourners and a young widow. "Every morning a law enforcement officer awakes and says to himself, 'There but for God go I.' Our brother died doing what he wanted, and he did it so well we can all stand in the light he shed."

Jerry Johnson spoke after the chief and told about how eager and ready for the vice job Larry was. "Larry did his job well," he said. "He was truly dedicated." After the service, Kindice led the honor guard to the grave site and saluted as the casket passed by on its way to the final resting place.

Taps were played, and the honor guard took the flag from Bullock's casket and folded it. Chief Kindice took the flag and presented it to Brenda. "Please accept this flag in honor of a brave and dedicated man."

McCombs was convicted of second-degree murder and sentenced to sixty years. Many community activists, led by McCombs's father, advocated for his freedom. They argued that the police had been dressed in street clothes and had not properly identified themselves. McCombs, they said, had thought it was a home invasion and had shot out of self-defense. The argument had not been enough to keep him from being convicted of the crime, but in 1988, McCombs was released on parole after having served thirteen years in prison. The death of Bullock did lead to much discussion of the use of plainclothes vice officers, a debate that remains relevant today and will continue into the future. Unfortunately, Larry Bullock is no longer with us to weigh in. He was by all accounts an officer who would have continued to rise in the ranks and would have had a deep impact on the future of policing in Durham, but he was taken away from his family and his community much too soon.

Durham police chief Jon Kindice spoke highly of Investigator Larry Bullock during his eulogy and defended his department's tactics. *From the Durham Sun.*

THE STILL UNSOLVED MURDER
OF AUBREY GOSS

Aubrey Goss was a really good guy by all accounts—a good dad and a good neighbor. Aubrey never hurt anyone as far as anyone knew, but he made a habit of breaking state alcohol laws. By 1976, he had been convicted thirteen times for liquor law violations. That record wasn't bad since he had been charged with forty violations throughout that period. Making moonshine and selling it had been a career that Aubrey seemed to have been born for. By October 1976, Aubrey was operating a liquor and gambling establishment above a garage on Driver Street in Durham. A heavy steel door kept anyone out whom Aubrey did not want inside, and he kept a pistol by the bar.

In the early morning hours of October 7, 1976, Johnny Goss, who lived beside the garage, saw a strange car in the driveway of the garage. He could see that it was a small white car, maybe a Ford Pinto, but he couldn't tell for sure. The light that was usually on the outside of the garage was off. Johnny was a business partner as well as the brother of Aubrey, and he was familiar with the guests who frequented the garage. He looked at the clock on the table beside his bed at 3:30 a.m. He rubbed his eyes and yawned. Whoever it was, he knew that Aubrey had it under control. It could be a new customer, or someone could just have gotten a new ride. He wasn't concerned about it and went back to bed. He would later regret not taking a better look at the car or getting up and walking next door.

Johnny was awakened early the next morning by one of their frequent customers, who said that he couldn't get in. At 8:00 a.m., he walked next door and up the stairs to the apartment. When he opened the door, he was shocked at the carnage that he saw. His brother lay on the floor in a pool of blood, another man was hunched forward in a chair and a third man was lying on a bed in the corner. All were dead from brutal wounds. Johnny retreated down the stairs and called the Durham Police Department.

The police identified the three victims as Aubrey Goss, Nick Wheeler and Walter Dean. Goss had been shot in the back, stomach and head eight times from two different caliber guns. He was also stabbed three times in the back. It appeared that he had opened the steel security door for someone, most likely two people, and they had opened fire on him immediately as he tried to flee back into the apartment. Walter Dean, who was a regular at the apartment and helped out around the establishment when he could to get free liquor, was found hunched forward in the chair, having been stabbed multiple times and struck in the head with a heavy blunt object. Lying on a bed in the corner was Nick Wheeler, who was killed by heavy blows to the head and stab wounds to both the front and back of his body. It appeared to investigators that the blunt object that they had been struck with had been a hatchet.

The murders were absolutely brutal and baffled the police. Goss was an illegal liquor kingpin and was known to law enforcement, but he didn't have any known enemies. He might have crossed someone, and they sought revenge. There was no indication of any family problems or of any fights that had taken place in the previous days and weeks. It was also possible that it was a robbery. Goss was known to carry a large amount of cash with him, but when he was found, his wallet was empty. He was obviously robbed of the money he had, but robbery as a motive was tricky. The murders were just too brutal for a simple robbery, and the two men present in the apartment were small men. Both weighed about 110 pounds and were described by the police as "harmless alcoholics." Why would they be slain so brutally just for being there?

The investigators found few clues. A half-drunk beer bottle was below the stairs leading up to the apartment, and another was at the bottom of the stairs. A dime was also found near tire tracks in the garage, but it was difficult to determine if these were related to the murderer or just a part of the regular comings and goings of the establishment. The suspect list was difficult too. The police began to compile a list of people who frequented the garage, but they found that since it was not a legal establishment, they were dealing with shady people, all of whom seemed to have some criminal history. One after another, they brought in anyone who could give them any information, but the trail ran cold. It would remain cold for decades.

In 2005, seemingly out of the blue, two arrests were made in the 1976 murders on Driver Street: Ronnie Manning and Gary "Whitley" Bennett. The arrests were made on the testimony of a witness who said that they had been reluctant to come forward in 1976 because of Bennett's affiliation with the Hells Angels Motorcycle Club. Manning had been a suspect at the time, and the police had driven to his home at Atlantic Beach to conduct an interview but filed no charges at the time. The witness who had come forward in 2005 claimed to have seen the two men together in a white Pinto before the killings and then afterward in bloodstained clothes.

The evidence of the case hung on the testimony of one person: Jesse Lyle Ennis. Manning and Bennett submitted to lie detector tests and DNA testing, but no scientific evidence could be secured that would put them at the scene. Other accusations that claimed the men were guilty were not backed by evidence. By 2007, the Durham district attorney's case had fallen apart. Ennis recanted his testimony, then took back his recantation and then claimed the DA had offered him $10,000 for his testimony. The district attorney had no choice but to drop the charges on the two men and set them free.

The case is cold again and will most likely never be solved. If the two men were guilty, then the prosecutors in Durham would have to have very strong evidence to bring the charges again after the long, drawn-out process they went through between 2005 and 2007, which ended in dropping the charges. If it was not the two men, then the chances of finding all new evidence, or of the suspect still being alive, grow smaller by the day. For the victims and their families, the chapter will probably never have a conclusion. Aubrey Goss's family have stated many times since the murders that although he skirted the state's liquor laws, he was a good husband and father who has been missed immensely. Maybe one day a miraculous break in the case will lead to justice, or at least answers to the many questions that exist.

RANDOM SHOOTINGS OF 1976

The citizens of Durham, after Thanksgiving 1976, began to look toward the Christmas season and the end of the bicentennial year. Winter was setting in, and the air was becoming crisper as the days moved toward the yearly merriment, celebrated with parades, caroling and Santa Clause making his annual ride. The sand of the hourglass poured a steady stream, winding down to the dropping of the ball in Times Square and the fresh hope of a new year. Few would have thought that the picture-perfect conclusion of the year could be so brutally ripped to shreds. On December 10, a little after three o'clock in the afternoon, thirty-year-old Leroy Goldston worked his shift at the carwash on Angier Avenue. He was finishing up toweling off a Chevy when he was shot in the neck. The police searched the area but found no trace of the shooter or any witnesses. They chalked it up to a random act of violence but soon learned that there was a predator in their midst.

On the eighteenth, David Solomon, thirty-six, hustled out to the pump at the service station where he had just started his new job. It was his first day, and he was putting his best foot forward as he filled a lady's gas tank. He cleaned her windows while the pump worked and rushed to put the handle back and close her tank. He walked to the driver's window with a smile on his face. She returned the smile as she sat with her open purse on her lap, waiting for him to tell her the amount. As he opened his mouth to speak, though, a shot rang out and ripped into his hip, passing through his left hand.

He felt himself slam against the side of her car, and he slid down, conscience only of the pain and the screams coming from the driver's seat. He looked around at the buildings, trees and passing cars but could not see his would-be assassin.

A few days later, on December 19, Herbert Medlin, twenty-six, was walking down the street not far from the service station and car wash with his girlfriend, Annie. They held hands in the early dark of winter when, suddenly, from behind them a man stepped from the bushes between two houses and shot him in the back. He fell dead, and his girlfriend sank down beside him as he died, only seeing a brief glimpse of a man with a rifle disappear back into the foliage. The police determined that the shot had come from a .30-caliber rifle—the same caliber in the shootings of Leroy Goldston and David Solomon. The police were now dealing with a deranged individual with a high-caliber rifle who was seemingly shooting people at random.

At his home, Herbert Bradshaw, a sixty-eight-year-old retiree, sat at the dinner table with his wife. He had been an editor of the *Durham Herald Sun*, taught journalism at North Carolina State University in Raleigh and was a member of the Durham Redevelopment Commission. In his day, he had seen many crazy stories in Durham, but nothing to match this. A maniac was on the loose shooting strangers. What was the world coming to, he thought as his wife stood to clear the table.

"No, let me do it," he said as he reached out and touched her hand. She smiled and sat down as Herbert collected the dishes and took them to the sink. They continued to talk as he washed the dishes, and she sat at the dining room table sipping her after-dinner coffee. Herbert was a happy man, a man who had accomplished many of his dreams and looked forward to every day he could spend enjoying the fruits of all of his hard work for so many years. He looked out of the small window above the sink into the darkness of the night. His wife heard glass break and then a thud. She looked over into the kitchen and saw Herbert dead on the floor with a hole in the center of his forehead.

The city was a buzz with fear and angst as the days passed by. Chief of Police Jon Kindice held a news conference and advised residents to stay away from windows at night and to be mindful of their surroundings when out. They were following all leads but were waiting for a break in the case. They would get the break on December 22 when three young men were sitting outside a convenience store on Enterprise Street and a man across the street from them pulled out a pistol and began firing at them. They scattered, and the man fled after firing three shots at them.

The last of the random shootings of 1976 took place on the corner of Enterprise Street, where three men were sitting and talking when a gunman began firing on them from across the street. *Author's collection.*

The man had not used a rifle but was one of the police suspects nonetheless because of the similarities in the random nature of the attack. He was identified by the three young men as James Willie Grace. The police began looking for him and put out a picture of him to the press, who began to show it on the evening news.

By December 27, he was in custody. A Johnston County sheriff's deputy in Clayton, North Carolina, which is about ten miles outside Raleigh, had seen his picture on television and recognized him as someone he had dealt with in the past. He went back to the house where he had encountered Grace before, and he was there hiding out with a friend. The sheriff's deputy took him into custody without incident on a felony assault with a deadly weapon charge. He sat in the Clayton Police Station for six hours waiting to be taken to Durham and was as cool as a cucumber, law enforcement officers would later say.

With little concrete evidence to convict Grace, who was not admitting to anything, he was charged in connection with the shooting at the convenience store. He pleaded not guilty by reason of insanity. His mother testified that she had him committed to a mental institution in November right before the

The third Durham Courthouse around the time of the trial of James Willie Grace. *From the Durham Sun.*

shootings took place because he was found not competent to stand trial on a robbery charge. He was released six days later because the hospital deemed him not to be dangerous to himself or others. She said that he had been eating dog food and sleeping at the end of her bed at night. He told her he had to do that to stay safe from the other, imagined dogs in the house.

At his trial, District Attorney Anthony Branson said to the jury, "I grant you he's mentally ill, I grant you he is bizarre." The jury, despite his mental illness, found him guilty, and he was sentenced to twenty-four to thirty years in prison. The sniper shooting stopped with his arrest, but the families of the victims were never given the justice of seeing the shooter stand trial for the shootings. James Willie Grace was never tried for the shootings for lack of evidence and served his time in prison for the attempted murder on Enterprise Street. The sniper shootings remain officially unsolved to this day.

THE TRAGIC MURDER OF DARLENE TILLEY

September 14, 1980, was a warm day in Durham, North Carolina. Fall came late to the Tar Heel State, and the warm weather allowed kids to spend the long days of late summer outside. Darlene Tilley, a thirteen-year-old eighth grader at Chewning Junior High School, was spending the day playing softball at Glenn School field. Darlene was an unashamed tomboy who loved to play ball and be outside. She was more comfortable mowing the lawn than cleaning the house, and her parents appreciated her as the smart, loving girl she was.

After a long morning at play and a brief lunch, she had been at it all day. Around 4:30 p.m., she told her best friend, Tammy, that she was not feeling well and was going to head home. Tammy asked her if she wanted to walk her home, but Darlene said that she was fine and would go by herself. It was a decision that may have cost Darlene her life, or maybe it was a decision that saved her friend Tammy's life. No one will ever know.

Darlene set out toward her home on the gravel service road that ran alongside Interstate 85, which traverses the state from South Carolina up to Virginia. It was a quiet road with little traffic except for locals who either lived off the road or used it as a shortcut to somewhere, but the steady hum of cars came through the small line of trees hiding the road from the highway. It was here, less than three hundred yards from her house, that Darlene was last seen alive.

When she did not come home, her parents did as most parents would and called anywhere she could be. They called the police and their pastor at Bible

A morning of softball and spending time with her best friend was how Darlene Tilley spent her last hours before her tragic death. *Author's collection.*

Baptist Church, where they were active members and were overwhelmed with help looking for Darlene. Men walked through the woods near the house and checked the area around the field at Glenn School and all around the Gorman community of Durham. She was nowhere to be found.

The Sheriff's Department employed various methods over the next few weeks in its search for Darlene. Officers searched on foot through the community and brought in a state-owned helicopter to search the area from the sky. Their initial thought was that she was a runaway, but they quickly changed their opinion as they spoke with her family, friends and church leaders. They all insisted that Darlene was a happy, loving child who was close to her parents and family. She had given no sign of there being any friction in her home life.

No matter what methods law enforcement employed, though, they seemed to run into walls everywhere they went. Donnie Tilley, Darlene's father, scraped together $1,000 to offer up as a reward for any information that would help them find his daughter. Weeks into the investigation, the Sheriff's Department had no leads other than rumors. One rumor was that Darlene

Thicket where the body of Darlene Tilley was found. *From the* Durham Sun.

Sheriff Bill Allen (*second from right*) led the investigation for the disappearance and then murder of Darlene Tilley. *From the* Durham Sun.

had an altercation of some kind with an individual who was on staff at Bible Baptist Church, but they could not confirm anything. There was some concern about the people of the Gorman community, which was a tight group, protecting others who were pillars of the community and seemingly untouchable. Whether there was nothing there or the person was protected, the authorities had nothing until Saturday, November 15.

Kevin Eubanks, a local man, along with two of his friends were hunting in the area between Red Mill Road and Snow Hill Road about nine miles from Darlene Tilley's house. They were moving along a gravel road that circled a soybean field when they saw what looked like bones in the thicket. They moved closer and saw what were obviously human remains, and they immediately left and called the Sheriff's Department. When the remains were examined, they were so decomposed that it was not possible to tell the age, race or gender of the body.

The autopsy examination, with the help of dental records, revealed that the body was that of Darlene. It was determined that she had died of blunt-force trauma to the head and had suffered several stab wounds. It was impossible to tell if she had been abused in any other way because of the state of her body.

A sense of sadness descended over the Gorman community. This little girl, who was so full of life and such a blessing to her family, was gone for good. The feelings of worry and not knowing were replaced by the immense feeling of loss and sadness. Her mother worried about things like Darlene's fear of the dark and wondered if she was eating and being taken care of. Those worries faded as she said goodbye to her daughter and mourned.

Durham County Sheriff Bill Allen vowed to continue the search for the killer, but weeks, months and then years passed without any breaks in the case. She was never forgotten, though, and even many decades later, friends of Darlene will occasionally call the Sheriff's Department and remind them of their commitment to the investigation into her death. The hope is that someone somewhere will decide to give some bit of information or some piece of evidence that will lead to an arrest and an eventual conviction—at long last securing justice for the murder of Darlene Tilley.

CONFLICTING TESTIMONIES

Sergeant D.M. Laeng, a public safety officer, was on his normal patrol shortly after midnight on a cold Tuesday night in February 1982. The headlights of his patrol car cut through the darkness, illuminating the stone sign to Duke Park. The park was nestled in the woods off Roxboro Road and was a lively spot in the summer. Families came and used the pool to cool down and the stone picnic shelter to relax and get in the shade. In the wintertime, it was not as busy, and Laeng wanted to check it out and make sure that everything was as it should be. He pulled into the driveway to make sure that no drifters or homeless people were sleeping in the park or, more likely, young lovers looking for a place where they could have some privacy. As he pulled through, he noticed a shoe and a pocketbook on the ground brightened by the headlights of his patrol car. Sergeant Laeng pulled his car up to the items and got out. He shined his flashlight down on them and then scanned the area, sweeping the beam across the trees and bushes. In the nearby picnic shelter, he saw a man lying on one of the picnic tables.

Sergeant Laeng walked toward the picnic shelter, and as he came closer, he saw that the man was sleeping hard with some clothes under his head as a pillow. He shined the light around the shelter and saw more clothes lying on a nearby table. He shined the light back down on the man's face.

"Wake up," Laeng said as he nudged the sleeping man, who opened his eyes and looked up with surprise at the officer. "You can't be here son," Laeng said as he continued to scan the area and the young man sat up on the table. Laeng's light cut through the night as he looked around the shelter.

Duke Park, once the home of a large city pool, is still a busy spot in Durham, although the pool has long been filled in and a playground built over it. *Author's collection.*

It stopped on a pile of lumber a few feet away, and he could see the battered and beaten body of a woman. He didn't know it at the time, but it was the body of thirty-five-year-old Cynthia Easterling. His hand went instinctively to his revolver, and he took a step back from the man. He shined his light back on him and saw that he was casually waking up while rubbing his eyes and grumbling about not having a place to stay. He was seemingly oblivious to the dead woman just feet away from them.

"Stand up for me," Laeng ordered, and the man complied. "Turn around and put your hands behind your back." Other than the continued griping

The body of Cynthia Easterling was found among construction debris behind the picnic shed. *Author's collection.*

about just sleeping there and not bothering anyone, he complied with the officer. Laeng took him to the squad car and put him in the backseat. It was almost as if he had no idea she was there. Laeng called in to dispatch on the radio and explained the situation. He had a body and one in custody at Duke Park. The man in the back seat, suddenly alert, began to talk fast. Sergeant Laeng paid him no mind as he got back out of the car and moved back toward the shelter and potential crime scene. The man would have plenty of time to tell someone his story, but now was not the time.

His name was Thomas Carter, and he was twenty-four years old when he fell asleep on the picnic table. Recently discharged from the army for being AWOL, he had been working as a plumber's helper since coming home to Durham. When he got to the station and was questioned by detectives, he claimed that he had been kicked out of his brother's house and was homeless. He had been bouncing from place to place since he returned to Durham. He had spent a few nights in the park a few days before, then a motel and then his brother's house. He told the police he had come to the picnic shelter at around 10:00 p.m. He took some damp clothes out of his duffel bag and hung them up and then took other clothes not as wet and made himself a pillow. He picked up a stick that he found in the shelter and put it beside him under the picnic table in case he had any trouble. Carter was adamant that he had no idea the body of Cynthia Easterling lay just feet from him outside of the shelter. He swore that he had never even heard of Cynthia Easterling or seen her before.

The evidence at the scene told a different story. Her body was about thirty feet from him in a lumber pile right outside the picnic shelter. The wet clothes hanging up had been washed in the pool, and blood stains still were on the garments. The "stick" that Carter had picked up was actually the leg of a chair and was clearly the murder weapon. Cynthia was nude from the waist down, and it was believed that she had been sexually assaulted. Thomas Carter was booked on murder charges.

He was joined soon after by another suspect. Mark Allen Upchurch was also arrested for the murder of the Durham native. Days after the arrest of Carter, an inmate in the Durham County Jail asked one of the jailers if he could speak to the sheriff. He was taken out by one of the deputies and told them that they needed to check Upchurch's car for items from the recently murdered Easterling. He had been heard by several inmates saying that Carter was innocent and claiming to have known Easterling and who killed her. When the police searched his car, they found a shirt spattered with blood that matched Cynthia's. They also linked a belt buckle found at the scene to Upchurch.

The men were tried separately, with Carter going first. He stuck to his story of not having anything to do with the murder. As far as he was concerned, he was at the wrong place at the wrong time. He actually called Upchurch as a witness hoping that he would testify, as he had told the other inmates, that Carter was innocent. He was surprised though.

Upchurch had changed his story several times while in jail. By the time he took the stand in the trial of Thomas Carter, his testimony laid the blame for the senseless murder of Cynthia at the feet of Carter. He testified that he and Easterling had been drinking the day of the murder and driving around. This was confirmed by witnesses, but Upchurch said that they were not alone. He said they had stopped and were sitting and talking in his car when Cynthia spotted someone she knew. She called out of the car window to the man whom she called "Spooky," and he came up to them. Upchurch said that this man was Carter. He had gone along with them drinking, and they ended up at Duke Park. Upchurch claimed that Easterling and Carter had begun to argue, and Carter attacked her and beat Easterling with a wooden chair leg. That, he said, was the reason he had her blood spattered on his shirt. Upchurch testified that he fled the scene.

Carter's defense was dumbfounded that he had hung the crime squarely on their client, but the damage was done. Carter was convicted of second-degree murder, but he only served fifteen years in prison. Mark Allen Upchurch was able to avoid jail time for the murder despite the evidence of his involvement in the crime. Cynthia Easterling became just another victim, a statistic, but she was much more than that to those who loved her. The tragic death she experienced is an example of how important it is to be able to tie evidence together and weave it into a compelling argument for a jury. Only Cynthia knows the whole story and if justice was served.

MURDER OF CINDY KIRK

August 21, 1989, was a hot day in Durham when Cindy Kirk took a last look down at her sleeping daughter, Suzanne, in her crib. She glanced at the clock on the wall as she grabbed her purse and the baby's pink diaper bag. She was a supervisor at the Liggett & Meyer Tobacco Company and had to work the second shift. Suzanne had to go to the babysitter until her husband, Bill, could pick her up after he got off work. When she opened the side door, the heat and humidity hit her, contrasting the cool air in her house.

Suzanne's babysitter peered through the blinds of her house, looking out for Cindy's car to pull in her driveway. It was not like her to be late, and she was getting worried. She knew she had to be at work soon, so she called Cindy's house, but there was no answer. She hung up and called Cindy's sister, Beverly, who lived nearby. Beverly was worried too, and after trying to call her sister herself, she drove to her house. She was sure something bad had happened to Cindy, so when she pulled into the driveway and saw blood on the concrete, she flagged down the neighbor and asked him to check the house.

He walked toward the house and the side door, where he knew Cindy and Bill came and went most often. He began to see what appeared to be blood leading to the door and blood along the banister going up the four stairs. The metal screen door was closed, but he could see that the door to the kitchen was opened. He cautiously peered inside and saw the lifeless body of Cindy lying in a pool of blood on the kitchen floor. He stumbled backward and ran into his house to call the police.

When they arrived, they found that she was indeed dead. The officers moved cautiously through the house with guns drawn, not sure if the killer still lurked behind a corner or in a closet. The only other person they found in the house was little Suzanne, sleeping in her crib—unaware that her beloved mother had been stolen from her just a short time before. They immediately began to investigate the crime scene. Bill was contacted, and his whereabouts for the day were verified so he was quickly ruled out as a suspect.

The police found the purse and the diaper bag locked in her car unmolested. Bill walked through the house and confirmed that nothing was missing, so they were able to eliminate robbery as a motive. Neighbors were interviewed. One neighbor said the last time she saw Cindy, she was standing in the driveway talking to a clean-cut man. Another neighbor said that she heard a scream at about 1:30 p.m. but assumed that it was a child who had fallen down and gotten hurt. A landscaper told the police that he saw an olive-green Chrysler with a CB radio antenna on the back. The car was driven by a middle-aged white man. His description of the man driving the car was the same as the neighbor who had seen Cindy speaking to a man in her driveway. No one had seen the actual attack though.

The police determined that when Cindy came out of the house, she had locked her purse and the diaper bag in the car and was confronted by someone in her driveway. They pieced together that she didn't feel like she was in any danger since she was seen talking casually with the man. The police think that the suspect had driven by the house and asked her a simple and innocent question like asking for directions. They thought that Cindy, as she was giving him the directions, was at some point suddenly and viciously attacked. She had a defensive wound on her right hand that almost severed her thumb. The earring from her left ear was found in the driveway, having been ripped from her ear in the struggle. She had been stabbed five times, and from all the evidence, after the brutal attack, the killer did not pursue her. He simply turned back to his car and coolly drove away.

Cindy, on the other hand, had turned back toward the house. No one can know for sure what was going through her mind in her final moments as she stumbled toward the side door. As she retreated, though, it can be assumed that she was thinking of reaching safety in her home from the attacker, but also it can be assumed that she was moving herself in between the monster that had attacked her and her baby girl sleeping soundly inside.

The Durham Police Department immediately began to interview suspects from Cindy's inner circle of friends and family but came up with no information that they could use to find the killer. A $50,000 reward was offered, which in 1989 was a very substantial amount of money. The police followed more than two hundred leads, but they all ran into dead ends. Frustration grew for the family and the community as they tried to wrap their minds around how someone could murder her in broad daylight in front of her home and then just drive away with no witnesses. Speculation around what kind of killer this was ran wild through the city. Would he strike again?

Despite the rewards and the many leads, the police were stumped. They even went to the home where she had been slain and recorded Durham police officers re-creating the murder in the hopes that seeing a visual representation would jog someone's memory, but still nothing. Today, more than thirty years have passed since that brutal August afternoon, but the case is still unsolved and now cold. The fear of a homicidal maniac killing women in their driveways never became a reality, thankfully. But the lack of other killings just makes the case more baffling to the police. Although cold, the case remains open, and the Durham police will still follow any leads that they are given to bring the killer to justice.

COLDBLOODED

Sylvester Thompson Jr. had not been in Durham long. In fact, it had been less than five months since he left his home in Columbia, South Carolina, to try his luck in a different zip code. He had gotten his job at the BP station on Chapel Hill Boulevard soon after he got into town and had been working sometimes seven nights a week on the overnight shift there. It was not the best job, but it was a job, and he tried his best to do a good job until something better came along.

On the morning of August 25, 1998, Sylvester was mopping the floor of the BP station. It had been a pretty slow night, and he was trying to get ahead of his nightly tasks when a man burst through the doors pointing a gun at him. He demanded Sylvester open the cash register, and he complied. Security camera footage would later show him dropping the mop and going behind the counter to the cash register. He opens the drawer, takes out the till and lays it on the counter. Sylvester steps back from the counter to give the robber space to take whatever he wants.

The man with the gun takes the bills from the till as he stares at Sylvester standing back with his hands up. He then raises his weapon, fires two shots into Sylvester's chest, turns and walks away. Sylvester slumps down onto the floor and tries to make a call by pulling the phone from the counter to the floor by the cord, but before he can dial 911, he dies. He is found a few minutes later by a group of customers who come in and call the police. The police respond to the scene, and after looking at the surveillance and doing some investigation, they find that the killer is someone they are very familiar with: Gregory Gibson.

Sylvester Thompson Jr. was gunned down in cold blood while working at this gas station. *Author's collection.*

He was taken into custody and charged with first-degree murder. As he sat in his cell at the Durham County courthouse, many wondered how he could have even been allowed to have been a free man in the first place. He had, in fact, been a history maker, changing the law in North Carolina in regards to how minors are charged with crimes. He was destined to make even more history, although that would have also been a surprise as he awaited trial.

In 1992, Gibson was a thirteen-year-old seventh grader at Rogers-Kerr Middle School. Even then, he was no stranger to the law. Two years earlier, he had been arrested for larceny and breaking and entering. People who knew him would give differing opinions of the young man. He was not a bad student and made As and Bs, but many considered him a bully and a braggart. He could be a sweet kid and a pain in the butt to his teachers all in the same day.

It has been said that everyone in life comes to a crossroads and makes the decision of what kind of life they will live. Gibson came to that crossroad and made his decision on the night of June 16, 1992, at the home of ninety-year-old Mary Haddon. She was a small woman in stature, standing less than five feet tall, but was a much bigger personality. She loved playing bridge and sat on a pillow so she could look the other, taller players in the eyes as she played. She was known for hiring neighborhood kids to do work around her house, so this may be how she first came into contact with Gregory Gibson.

No one knows for sure, but what is known is that on that June night, Gibson decided that he wanted to take himself and his friends out on a joyride and decided to take Mary's 1970 Oldsmobile Cutlass. He broke into her house and demanded her keys. Mary, startled and scared, showed that she had more fight in her than he thought and refused to give him the keys. Gibson attacked her with a ball-peen hammer and beat her viciously. Then he retrieved a garden mattock and struck her several more times with it.

After the brutal and savage killing of Mary Haddon, he spent the rest of the night joyriding in her car and showing off to his friends. He was quickly picked up and became the youngest person in the history of the state of North Carolina to be charged with murder. Because he was thirteen and not fourteen, he couldn't be tried as an adult and was tried in juvenile court. He was found guilty but could only be sentenced to the maximum of confinement until his eighteenth birthday, at which time he would be released and his record cleared. Gibson was sent to C.A. Dillon Training School in Butner, North Carolina, for the next five years. While he was there, many people went to work to change the law. They saw that in the case of Gregory Gibson, the crime had been so vicious that the thought of him walking free was terrifying to most. The law was changed to allow prosecutors the ability to charge thirteen-year-olds as adults if the crime justified a harsher sentence.

In 1996, Gregory Gibson walked out of the juvenile detention center where he had lived for the past five years. He had a fresh start and a clean record as he began his adult life, but he quickly proved that he had already chosen his direction in life. He soon came back into contact with law enforcement. Between his release and the night he walked into the BP station on Chapel Hill Boulevard, he was charged with trespassing, assault, attempting to steal a car and possession of stolen goods. After the murder of Sylvester Thompson, Gibson again was the subject of much conjecture among lawmakers, who wondered how he could have been released with no supervision at all.

The law was again changed, making it mandatory for offenders who were convicted as minors to be supervised for some time after their release to make sure that they were on the right track. In jail waiting for his trial, Gibson was not planning on waiting for his day in court. In the early morning hours, the jail guard noticed that the small glass window of cell 43, where Gibson was locked up, was covered with tissue, blocking his view inside. He had just passed by six minutes before, and nothing seemed out of the ordinary. The guard opened the cell door and found Gibson hanging with a sheet around his neck from the bars covering the window. He tried to revive him, as did the EMTs who responded, but it was no use. Gregory Gibson was dead at the age of twenty years old.

In his young life, he had killed two innocent people and committed countless crimes of varying degrees of severity. He had been responsible for two laws being changed due to his actions. His death by hanging was the first in a chain of twelve suicides at the Durham County Jail, which in 2017 prompted Sheriff Mike Andrews to remodel the cells and take away any structure that would allow inmates to hang themselves in the future. Gregory Gibson, who lived a wicked, evil life, may have been in some way involved in saving someone else's life long after he took his own.

THE SUMITOMO SHOOTINGS

It had been more than six hours since the terror had begun on the campus of the Sumitomo Electric Fiber Optic Corporation in the Research Triangle Park. Sheriff's deputies had responded, and the SWAT team had arrived. They searched every square inch of the large building where the killer had entered. Everyone knew who it was. They knew the first moment the shots began. Even people who had not seen anything but followed the crowd fleeing the building shouted to others as they fled and hid behind cars. "It's Ladislav! It's Ladislav!" The thing that they had feared, the nightmare that many had dreaded, became reality on April 13, 1994.

Ladislav Antalik worked for a company contracting at Sumitomo in the Research Triangle Park. He was an immigrant from Czechoslovakia who came to the United States in 1988. He left behind a family in his homeland and a job as a military police officer to move to America and try to make it. He struggled from the very beginning. He had a very thick accent and had difficulty learning English. Even with help finding work and a place to stay by members of Our Lady of Lourdes Catholic Church in Raleigh, he still struggled.

In 1991, he pulled a knife on a roommate over a recorded message on the answering machine and was arrested. The roommate told police that he was so easily set off that it made it difficult to be around him. The charges were dropped because the roommate moved out and decided that it was not worth the hassle of going to court since Ladislav was no longer in his life. Later that year, he ran into a tree and was found by police still in the car, slumped over the wheel. He was charged with a DWI and lost his license. To make matters worse for Ladislav, he found out that his wife had no intentions of following him to the United States with his daughter.

Father Ingham of Our Lady of Lourdes later said of Antalik, "Generally speaking, people who come here as refugees are determined to create a better life for themselves. They're people with a certain desire and ambition, he seemed to lack those qualities. I found that unusual. A lot of the refugees we help have some desire to be part of the American dream. He didn't seem to have that." Ingham said also that "he was always rather sullen and appeared to be depressed." That sentiment would be expressed over and over again by people who knew and worked with him in the years leading up to the horrible events at Sumitomo.

Ladislav came to work at Sumitomo through contracted employment with a company named Litespeed Inc., which had a partnership with Sumitomo and AT&T. He immediately ran into conflict with his coworkers, who found him hard to speak with about work tasks because of his heavy accent and his short temper. He especially had trouble with one of his coworkers, Flora Jones. They had many disagreements, and both had gone to management to try to settle their disputes. The company wrote it off as a "cultural dispute," but it bothered Flora immensely having such tension at her job every day. She came home many nights tired and stressed because she just could not find a way to get along with Antalik. He was hard to understand and flew off the handle immediately if she asked him to repeat himself. Also, it seemed difficult for him to work with women, especially a Black woman. He seemed to bristle at everything she said to him, even more than he did with everyone else. Ladislav had even gone to management and complained that he was being made fun of for his accent.

In August 1993, Ladislav Antalik resigned from his position, citing interpersonal problems. Coworkers breathed a sigh of relief when they heard that he was gone, but they were surprised when he showed up for work the next day and had to be escorted off the Sumitomo campus by Durham County sheriff's deputies. He was almost forgotten by his former coworkers over the next few months as they continued their work in a more peaceful environment without Ladislav there.

On a rainy Wednesday morning in April of the following year, a car pulled up to the security booth and flashed an employment badge. It proceeded through the gates and parked in a visitor's space in the front. Out of the car stepped Ladislav Antalik, wearing a company smock and a name badge he walked toward the front door of Building C, where he used to work. He walked straight to the workstation of Flora Jones, who looked up from her work at him in a moment of terror as he raised a pistol he had taken from his pocket and shot her. When the first shots rang out, another employee pulled a fire alarm, and people began to flee the building. He shot three people as he proceeded through the building, one in the hall on the way to where he used to work and then two in their offices as he passed by. As people began to realize what was happening, many of them fled, and many hid in the building. Those outside the building hid behind their cars and waited for help to come.

Durham County sheriff's deputies arrived first, began to assess the situation and bravely entered the building looking for the shooter. He seemed to have vanished. They began the process of getting everyone out to safety. They found two wounded victims and got them outside to waiting ambulances. Two victims were found dead. Flora Jones had been murdered first. John Roblee, who was looking forward to celebrating his daughter's eighteenth birthday that night, was shot and killed in his office. The SWAT team arrived and took over the clearing of the building. Ladislav had shed his coat, hat, glasses and a .22 revolver as he walked through the building.

It took them more than six hours to find him. He had gone to the top floor and had put a bullet in his head behind a bookcase. The community and the workers were shocked. Flora Jones's husband, who had heard of the shooting on the news, stood crying outside of the building, knowing even before he was told that his wife had been killed by the man who had tormented her for so long. His motive seemed to be frustration and mental illness. In his apartment, a handwritten note was hanging on the refrigerator by a magnet that said, "Surviving!!! Death is the ultimate limit of all things."

As the mourning process took place, the issue of security and workplace violence came into the public conscience. The murders had not been the first in the Research Triangle Park. In 1982, Leonard Avery, a Vietnam veteran who was mentally ill, entered a building where he worked at IBM near the Sumitomo site with a .30-caliber rifle and began shooting at people. He wounded one man, and as he rampaged, he killed Ralph Glenn, who had approached him trying to talk him out of what he was doing. Ralph Glenn was a good man and an associate pastor in Durham. He had stepped out from cover to try to calm Avery, but he was shot down in cold blood. After throwing several firebombs and fleeing, Avery was apprehended at a roadblock in Raleigh, where he tried to kill himself but failed.

The shootings brought to light the lack of security measures and the need to monitor employees' mental health at the Research Triangle Park and other large companies. In both cases, there was a disgruntled employee who was an obvious threat to those they worked with daily. But it seemed to be brushed off by company management. Also, the lack of security on the company campuses was evident. In both situations, an armed man was able to get through security and enter into unlocked buildings. Changes had to be made, and they were. Doors were locked, security was tightened and counseling was offered to employees. Management received training on responding to reports of disgruntled employees or people who may have been showing signs of mental illness, and procedures were put into place to deal with workplace violence. All of these measures were good, but they were too late for the victims of Ladislav Antalik and Leonard Avery.

MURDER ON TERRY ROAD

O n the night of August 21, 1995, after his shift at the Philly Steak and Subs in Murrayville, North Carolina, rising Laney High School senior Danny Pence decided to ride out to the Johnny Mercer Pier in Wrightsville Beach to see what was going on. The pier was a place where local teenagers hung out, and everyone was looking to have some fun before school got back in session.

Danny drove his prized possession, a 1987 Black Ford Mustang, that his parents had gotten him when he turned sixteen. Danny had worked hard and made several improvements to the car, including a new paint job, a stereo system and wheels. He had been thinking about selling it to buy a motorcycle recently and figured that he would put the word out at the pier to see if anyone was interested. He had no way of knowing the danger that it would bring him.

At the pier was a twenty-year-old drifter from Wrightsville Beach named Todd Boggess and his fourteen-year-old runaway girlfriend, Melanie Gray, from Durham. They had spent the day under the pier smoking marijuana and drinking. Somewhere in the day, Melanie had told Todd that she wanted a Mustang one day, and when Todd heard through the grapevine of teenagers at the pier that night, he went to work immediately planning to steal the car from the handsome young man who owned it.

Todd approached Danny about buying the car, and Danny took him to the parking lot to take a look at it. Todd offered to buy the car from Danny and even offered him $1,000 over the asking price if he let him drive it to

Chockowitiny in Beaufort County to get the money. He told Danny that his parents had the money, but they lived out in the middle of nowhere because they were militia members and did not want to be around anybody. Danny agreed, and off they went heading north with Todd in the driver's seat, Danny riding shotgun and Melanie in the back.

Todd drove to an isolated place in the woods near Chocowinity and pulled over. He told Danny they would have to walk from there because he was afraid his parents would think they were feds trying to spy on them. When they got Danny out of the car, Todd and Melanie jumped back in and tried to drive off, leaving him behind, but Todd drove the car into a ditch and got stuck. Danny caught up with them and told them he didn't want to be left in the woods by himself and agreed to go with them. Danny even helped them get the car out of the ditch before being tied up and blindfolded. He had no way of knowing what cruel fate awaited him or he would have surely fought with all he had.

They drove through the night to northern Durham, where, off Terry Road, they found an abandoned house. They took Danny inside, and suddenly Todd began to punch him. In his confession later, Todd would say that he had no intentions of killing Danny, but when he would not go down, he just snapped. Todd pried up a floorboard and began hitting Danny in the head and the legs in an attempt to break them and prevent an escape. It was unnecessary, as the beating had taken the young man's life already.

Back home, Danny's mother was beside herself with worry and had reported him missing. The New Hanover Sheriff's Department was already working on it and had spoken to witnesses who said they had seen Todd Boggess and his girlfriend leave with him the night before from the pier. Todd and Melanie were seen on August 22 driving down Terry Road and then selling car speakers and a socket set that Danny's father had bought him at a pawn shop in Durham. By noon, a group of teenage boys had come across the battered body of Danny in the abandoned house and reported it.

The different agencies across North Carolina worked together quickly to get the information out and connect the dots. Todd and Melanie were officially on the run. In Beaufort County, the sheriff's department kept an eye on the house of Todd Boggess's mother in Chocowinity. On August 24, a deputy saw a 1987 Mustang, still bearing the license plate Danny had but spray-painted red with silver flames, in the driveway of the house. When Todd and Melanie spotted the deputy, they tried to run off, and a car chase ensued, with Todd driving into a corn field, ditching the car and hiding in

The body of Danny Pence was found in an abandoned house off Terry Road in North Durham. *Author's collection.*

the field. When a highway patrol helicopter appeared overhead, Todd and Melanie stepped out of the corn field with their hands up.

Their surrender started what would be over a decade-long series of trials and retrials. Attorneys for both Todd and Melanie pushed back against prosecution. Melanie, being fourteen, received a lighter sentence and, after a long list of infractions in prison, was released in 2005. Todd Boggess was found guilty in his first trial where tapes of his confession were played. His voice can be heard saying, "I feel like if I get the gas chamber, I know I deserved it. I believe that's what should have happened to me." His father, a convicted sex offender, in hopes of saving the life of his son, testified that he had sexually abused Todd and his older brother for years when they were children. Despite this, Todd was sentenced to death, but over the next decade, his conviction was overturned due to judicial errors in his first trial. He was retried and found guilty in 2006 and sentenced to life in prison.

It was as final a closure as the family of Danny Pence would get. After years of reliving the most horrible event of their lives, there was some measure of final justice for Danny. Nothing that the courts could have doled out would bring the bright young man back or fill the void of his absence to those who loved him and to the many who will never know him. It was a truly senseless act of savagery and evil that is impossible to comprehend.

HATE CRIME

On February 17, 2004, Sean Ethan Owen bounced into the kitchen of his mom and stepdad's Franklinton, North Carolina house. His sister, Tiffany, was there making herself some breakfast when he came in. He seemed in a great mood, and when she asked why, he told her he was meeting someone. He had been communicating with another man on a gay chatroom and was supposed to meet him that day. He told her he had to go to work, which was at a cellular phone store on Creedmoor Road in Raleigh, and then he was going to drive over to Durham to meet a man he called Blue.

Sean told her that he would be back in a little bit, but after he left that day in his mom's 1998 burgundy Ford Contour, Tiffany never saw her brother alive again. She became concerned as day turned into night and he never came back home. Three days later, down a twenty-foot embankment at the Old Farm Park on the Eno River in Northern Durham, the body of a man was found floating in the water face down. He had been shot and beaten brutally, but his cause of death was determined to be drowning. The body was soon identified as that of Sean Owen.

Two more days passed before the Durham Police Department responded to a call of a burning car at 614 Shepard Street. They found the Ford Contour that Sean was last seen in smoldering and smoking, partially burned out. The fire was set with newspapers, and they found a broken necklace that belonged to Sean. The police went to work collecting evidence and speaking to people in the areas of the park and the burned car.

The police received a gift when they learned that a few days after the murder of Sean Owen, the Contour had been parked in the fire zone at Northern High School and had been booted by the school resource officer. The fine to remove the boot was paid by Jimetrus Harris, who quickly told the police upon investigation that he had retrieved the car for Matthew Taylor. On March 4, 2004, Taylor was arrested along with friends Deangelo Epps and Derrick Maiden. Finger-pointing began among the three men, and the story of what happened began to come together through the foggy murk of their differing stories.

It was determined that on the day of the murder of Sean, February 17, Epps met Maiden and Taylor at Taylor's grandmother's house in Durham to hang out and play video games. While there, Taylor told the others that he had been luring a gay man to Durham via a chatroom to rob him. He told them that he had lined up a meeting that day. Taylor grabbed a gun, and the three of them went to the community clubhouse to wait for Sean Owen.

When they got to the clubhouse, Sean was already there waiting for them. They loaded into the Contour and headed to a convenience store to buy a cigar they planned to use to smoke marijuana. After they bought the cigar, Taylor directed Sean to the Old Farm Park on the Eno, where Sean then said they had to get out of the car to smoke since it was his mother's car.

What happened next has been disputed by Taylor, Epps and Maiden. Sean began to walk toward a picnic table nearby when Epps pulled a gun out and shot him in the back of the head. Sean began to run for his life yelling, "Please don't do this to me." They gave chase, and he fell to the ground, where he was shot again and brutally beaten by the three assailants. They carried him to the nearby riverbank and pushed him down the steep drop-off into the water. They found the keys to the Ford on the ground and drove back to Taylor's grandmother's house.

As the evidence unfolded and the three men went to trial, Derrick Maiden decided to make a plea deal and was an integral part of the prosecutor's case against Taylor and Epps. After the trial, Derrick Maiden was sentenced to twelve years for second-degree murder because of his cooperation. Mathew Taylor was sentenced to life imprisonment without parole for his role in the murder, as was Deangelo Epps, whom the judge called "sickeningly opportunistic and atrocious" when he doled out the sentences.

Sean Ethan Owen's name is not as well-known as Matthew Shepard's, the young man who was killed in 1998, or trans man Brandon Teena, who was killed in 1993. Although his name is not often used in the same conversation as these other members of the LGBT community, he was a victim of the

Sean Owen was shot in the back as he ran toward the picnic shelter at Old Farm Park on the Eno. *Author's collection.*

His body was found at the bottom of this steep drop-off on the banks of the Eno River. *Author's collection.*

same style of hate crime that they were. Lured into what he thought was a meetup with another gay man, he was targeted as an easy mark to be robbed and killed by predators. His death has been an example used in the need for hate crime legislation across the United States in hopes of protecting others from these types of crimes.

THE SENSELESS MURDER OF JEJUAN TAYLOR

O n April 18, 2013, JeJuan Taylor, a nineteen-year-old Duke University employee, and two friends were enjoying a Saturday night in Durham when he started getting calls on his cellphone. His friends could tell that there was some intrigue and mystery in his voice as he cryptically discussed a meeting with someone at Duke Manor Apartments off LaSalle Street. He hung up and told them that he had to make a quick trip by the apartments to drop something off and then he would be back to their plans. They knew that JeJuan sometimes sold marijuana to a small group of people so they figured that was what the meeting was about. By 9:00 p.m., he was backing his silver Mercedes into an empty space at building 44, where he could see the person who had called him sitting on the stairs.

Hope Farely sat on the stairs of the Duke Manor Apartments watching the entrance and saw JeJuan drive in and back into a parking space. She was on her cellphone, nervously chatting to try to quiet the butterflies in her stomach. The butterflies were in anticipation of what she knew was about to transpire, but Taylor was unaware of it. Two men hid behind a burgundy car parked near Farley, and a gray Isuzu Rodeo sat a distance away, running with a getaway driver behind the wheel. Hope came up to the window of his car and nervously began to count out the money for the drugs: $200 in twenties. Taylor, along with his two friends, were suddenly surprised when she was flung out of the way and a gun was jammed into the window along with commands being screamed out to give up the drugs and

JeJuan Taylor was lured to Duke Manor Apartments, where he was robbed and murdered. *Author's collection.*

money. Taylor threw the car into drive and began to drive away when two gunshots rang out. Ears ringing, the passengers screamed as the car rolled across the parking lot into a fence, and they realized that JeJuan had been shot two times in the head and was dead.

The encounter had its origins earlier that very day when Hope was standing at a bus station and Thomas "Tom Tom" Clayton pulled up in his gray Isuzu Rodeo and offered her a ride. She knew him from her job at McDonald's. They drove to pick up Clayton's friend Timothy Moore, or "Little Mack," as Clayton referred to him, and Rakeem Best. They went to Best's apartment at Campus Crossing on East Cornwallis Road, where they hung out smoking weed and drinking. Somewhere in the course of the time while they were at the apartment, Farley was shown a gun, and the group talked about making some quick and easy money by robbing a drug dealer. The guys told Farley that they had tried to set up a robbery, but the drug dealer did not show up.

She suggested to them that she knew someone who would show up for her. JeJuan Taylor was someone she had bought marijuana from on occasion, and she had a small dispute with him. They had worked together before in fast food, and she had once left some items at his house. She claimed that things were missing when she retrieved her belongings, but JeJuan swore that he had nothing to do with it. Clayton said he knew him and had a similar experience. So, it was decided. They would have Hope call him and request a meeting to buy a small amount of marijuana. Originally, the meeting was to take place at a Cook-Out restaurant, but that fell through. Then the plan shifted to the apartment at Duke Manor.

Farley later testified that Clayton gave Moore a gun and told him to wait until Farley was buying the drugs, then Moore and Best would push her out of the way and rob him. He told him not to use the gun unless he had to. Clayton would be waiting in the getaway car. The plan went smoothly at first. When Best and Moore approached the car, they pushed Farley out of the way, and Moore stuck the gun in Taylor's face demanding the drugs and the money. Moore was taken by surprise when Taylor resisted, not by producing a gun himself but by trying to drive away with his arm still jammed in the car window. Taylor was a careful man and had purposely backed in just in case he needed to make a quick getaway. Moore fired two shots, and everyone scattered. Best and Farley ran to the waiting Rodeo, and Moore disappeared into the night.

No one was arrested that night for the murder, but over time, everything began to fall into place for the police. Witnesses had seen the Rodeo drive away, so when the police found the vehicle, word got around that they were looking for its owner. Hope Farley didn't wait for Clayton to be picked up. She turned herself in and told the police her story. Clayton and Best were soon in custody. Moore was arrested much later after he committed another murder and his palm print was matched from the door of JeJuan's car. All four were charged with murder and over the next five years were convicted to varying degrees for the crime.

THE DEATH OF JEJUAN Taylor and the conviction of Hope Farley, Rakeem Best, Clayton Thomas and Timothy Moore is a snapshot of the underlying problems that Durham deals with every day. Durham is a beautiful city with so many wonderful things to offer—gorgeous venues for events, parks and historical sites, museums and sports teams. It's known as a city of top medical facilities and home to one of the nation's top universities. All of these wonderful attributes cover a city that struggles with drugs and violent crime on a regular day-to-day basis. It is an attribute that the city would like to change but has struggled with since the first days of its founding. Maybe one day things will change as the city constantly tries to improve, but until then, Bull City's reputation will remain the same. It's a city that is on the move and growing but also a place where you lock your doors at night and look over your shoulder when you are walking to your car.

SOURCES

Books

Anderson, J.B. *Durham County: A History of Durham County, North Carolina.* Durham, NC: Duke University Press, 1990.

Kotch, S. *Lethal State: A History of the Death Penalty in North Carolina.* Chapel Hill: University of North Carolina Press, 2019.

Wise, J. *Durham: A Bull City Story.* New York: Cambridge University Press, 2002.

Newspapers

Columbia Record
Durham Herald
Durham Recorder
Durham Sun
Herald-Sun
The Independent
Raleigh Times

Websites

Open Durham—Preservation Durham. opendurham.org.

ABOUT THE AUTHOR

 Rick Jackson is a native North Carolinian who grew up in Durham and now lives with his family in Wake Forest, just outside Raleigh. He currently teaches business and economic courses to high school students after spending many years in banking and finance in various positions. He has always had a passion for history and the stories of the people who lived it. He holds a bachelor's degree in history from Campbell University and an MBA from the University of Mount Olive. Rick enjoys traveling around North Carolina with his wife, Meghan, and their three children, Savannah, Ricky and Charlotte.

Visit us at
www.historypress.com